1979

Six French Poets of Our Time

PRINCETON ESSAYS IN LITERATURE
For complete listing, see page 201

Six French Poets of Our Time

A CRITICAL AND HISTORICAL STUDY

Robert W. Greene

Princeton University Press
Princeton, New Jersey

Publication of this book has been aided by a grant from
The Andrew W. Mellon Foundation
This book has been composed in VIP Garamond

Clothbound editions of Princeton University Press books
are printed on acid-free paper, and binding materials are
chosen for strength and durability.

Printed in the United States of America by Princeton
University Press, Princeton, New Jersey

for my parents,
Hugh Greene, *in memoriam*
and
Mary Lynch Greene
and for
Judith, Rachel and Sean

Preface

In this book I try to combine practical criticism with literary history. The criticism, though by turns descriptive and interpretive, ultimately favors the latter mode, since my main critical goal is to elucidate the poetic universes of a specific series of modern French writers. As literary history, the book's purpose is to trace the patterns forged through time by the interlocking nature of these universes. Implicit in this twofold intention is the belief that critical inquiry must first and foremost seek to illuminate and extend a product of the creative mind, the literary text. Enormous contributions to critical theory have been made in recent years by thinkers, based for the most part in Paris, who tend to reject any distinction between the critical and the creative intelligence. Thus, to maintain such a distinction in a book that deals with contemporary French poetry will no doubt strike the reader as ironic. There are deeper ironies involved here, however. There is also, for example, the fact that my own critical practice in this book draws upon some of the insights of these same French thinkers. But perhaps the book's largest paradox concerns its central thesis, which purports to demonstrate, among other things, the inseparability of the artistic and the analytical turn of mind in the cases of six twentieth-century French poets. Let these ironies, as hereby acknowledged, stand as a mark of my genuine esteem for those critics whose aim is "la connaissance des lois générales qui président à la naissance de chaque oeuvre" (T. Todorov, *Poétique*, p. 19), as well as for those who celebrate the advent of "un mode d'écriture nouveau, unitaire, global, où les distinctions de genres, radicalement abandonnées, laissent place à ce qu'il faut bien appeler des 'livres' " (P. Sollers, *Logiques*, p. 206). Let it be further noted that I too would discourage clearcut distinctions among the various genres, but perhaps especially when the writer in question is primarily a poet.

The choice of poets treated in this book—Pierre Reverdy, Francis Ponge, René Char, André du Bouchet, Jacques Dupin and Marcelin Pleynet—of course ultimately reflects my own tastes rather than any "objective" esthetic or historical criteria. Nevertheless, this particular grouping has, I believe, a validity or at least an appositeness that transcends personal preference. For by examining these figures consecutively one can follow the evolution of avant-garde currents in French poetry since 1910, and one can do so without either being swallowed up by Surrealism or denying to Surrealism its revolutionary impact on artistic, moral and political values. Studied chronologically, moreover, as they are here, these six poets may provide a useful reference axis for French poetry in general over the last sixty to seventy years.

Selecting the year 1910 as a *terminus ab quo* also represents a somewhat arbitrary choice on my part. But here too I think the decision can be justified in reasonably objective terms. Scarcely two years earlier, Cubism was "born," an event that signaled the greatest upheaval in painterly esthetics since the Renaissance and a movement that was to have an immediate, profound and lasting effect on French poetry. Four years later, the Guns of August brought that latter-day golden age, *la belle époque*, to a dramatic close. More directly relevant to the present circumstances is the fact that in October 1910, not long after his twenty-first birthday, Pierre Reverdy moved to Paris from his native Narbonne, arriving in the capital too late to fall under the exclusive sway of the aging Symbolists but just in time to feel the full impact of nascent Cubism. As for the wider resonance of the year 1910, regarding innovations in many domains of artistic and intellectual endeavor throughout Europe, suffice it at this point to recall (after Robert Alter in *Partial Magic*, pp. 138-39) Virginia Woolf's startling claim that "on or about December 1910 human nature changed."

Human nature may or may not have changed in late 1910, but from around that time onward French poetry at least would move, on an increasingly broad scale, in directions only hinted at in the most radically innovative texts of the Symbolist era.

Earlier versions of parts of this book have appeared as articles in scholarly journals. A section of chapter one was published, in an earlier draft, as "Pierre Reverdy, Poet of Nausea," in *PMLA*, 85 (January 1970), 48-55. Sections of chapter two appeared, in earlier versions, as "Francis Ponge, Metapoet," in *MLN*, 85 (May 1970), 572-92, and as "Encomium for Francis Ponge," in *Books Abroad*, 48 (Autumn 1974), 659-68. A previous draft of part of chapter three was published under the title "René Char, Poet of Contradiction," in *The Modern Language Review*, 66 (October 1971), 802-9. An earlier, shorter version of chapters four and five together appeared as "André du Bouchet and Jacques Dupin, Poets of *L'Ephémère*," in *French Forum*, 1 (January 1976), 49-67. Chapter six was published, in briefer form, as "Poetry, Metapoetry and Revolution: Stages on Marcelin Pleynet's Way," in *The Romanic Review*, 68 (March 1977), 128-40. Permission to reprint these articles, in revised and expanded form, is gratefully acknowledged.

The poems quoted in this book are reproduced by kind permission of the following publishers: Flammarion, for all Reverdy poems save "Drame"; Editions Gallimard, for those of Ponge, Char and Dupin; Mercure de France, for "Drame" by Reverdy and for Du Bouchet's texts; and Editions du Seuil, for Pleynet's. Full documentation for the quoted material appears in the body of the study and the notes.

It would be impossible for me to identify all the poets, critics and scholars whose writings have in one way or another helped me to begin to see how poetry functions. However, one such figure, Michael Riffaterre, perhaps looms larger than the rest as a source of enlightenment for me, and although it follows a path rather different from his, in its own small way this book is a tribute to Riffaterre's seminal work.

A number of individuals and organizations contributed significantly to the preparation of this book. Anne Greet Cushing, Raymond Federman and Carlos Lynes encouraged the project at its virtual inception, for which I am forever in their debt. For his continued interest in my work, including my research for the present book, and his many kindnesses through the years, I should like to thank François Chapon, curator of the collection at the Bibliothèque Littéraire Jacques-Doucet. Francis Ponge's chance reading of and receptiveness to my 1970 essay on his work in an important sense inspired me to carry the project to completion; the human being is fully as extraordinary as the writer and it gives me special pleasure to acknowledge my indebtedness to him. At successive stages in its long gestation, this study was first presented to my graduate students at Berkeley, Iowa and Albany. I am particularly beholden to these students for their willingness to join me in exploring relatively uncharted literary terrain and for their probing questions regarding that terrain. Both the research for and the writing of the book were greatly facilitated by grants-in-aid from the Research Council of the University of Iowa, the American Council of Learned Societies and the American Philosophical Society, for which I wish to express my heartfelt appreciation. Mary Ann Caws, Renée Riese Hubert, Reinhard Kuhn and Sarah N. Lawall read the entire manuscript and offered extremely helpful comments and suggestions concerning it; I am profoundly grateful to them for their generosity, their attentiveness and, not least, their moral support. I thank Marjorie Sherwood and Christine K. Ivusic of Princeton University Press for their interest in the manuscript and their thoughtful assistance with it on its way to publication. Finally, my deepest thanks go to my wife, Judith Kramer-Greene, whose intelligence, enthusiasm and gifted editor's eye are alone responsible for whatever cogency this study may possess.

Albany, New York   R.W.G.
May 1978

Contents

Six French Poets of Our Time

Introduction

French poets have for centuries shown remarkable lucidity concerning their art, as well as a continuous capacity for intelligent, extended discourse in its regard. From the time of the Pléiade down to the present day, moreover, manifestoes, *a posteriori* theorizing and other forms of esthetic speculation and self-scrutiny have played an extremely important part in the evolution of the genre. In our own century Paul Valéry perhaps more obviously than any other contemporary figure epitomizes this propensity of French poets for constant and perceptive self-analysis. Valéry's life and work also of course point toward a danger that, for the poet, can accompany hyper-lucidity or an obsessive preoccupation with theoretical matters—eventual paralysis in the realm of practice. On the other hand, when viewed in its entirety, Valéry's *oeuvre* makes manifest truths that are latent in Baudelaire and Mallarmé, that the critical and the creative faculties are inseparable and that in a truly great poet an artistic temperament can and often does co-exist with an intellectual temperament. Indeed, the principal lesson to be learned from Valéry may be that the poet who habitually monitors himself does not automatically foreshorten the pioneering thrust of his poetic enterprise. On the contrary, so Valéry's example ultimately suggests, by keeping one eye on the techniques, the mechanisms and the philosophical assumptions and implications that inform his work, a poet does the very thing that allows him to function and develop as a poet.

A number of twentieth-century French poets, most notably Valéry and several figures associated with the aggressively intellectual and increasingly Marxist-oriented review *Tel Quel* (which, interestingly enough, was named after one of Valéry's works), have expressed their esthetic concerns as freely in poems as in expository texts. In the cases of Francis Ponge, a frequent contributor to *Tel Quel* during the early and middle 1960's, and Marcelin Pleynet, a member of the review's editorial board since 1962, a programmatic refusal to maintain traditional genre distinctions accounts in part no doubt for their readiness to address themselves *to* poetry *in* poetry. Another factor behind this tendency on the part of at least these *telquelistes* is their radical contextualist stance, their rejection of referentiality in literary language. Poetry for them is not merely an appropriate "subject" for poetry, but each poem or text must focus upon its own occasion, its own terms. Every text must fold back metapoetically on itself, must explore its own genesis, its creative process and method. For Ponge specifically a poem is a "création métalogique,"[1] a Gidean "mise en abyme." Thus a profoundly analytical turn of mind links the neo-Classical generation of Valéry and Gide to Ponge and Pleynet, a turn of mind that blurs the frontier between imaginative and speculative writing, or, broadly speaking, between poetry and philosophy.

But French poets have rarely drawn a sharp distinction between poetry and philosophy. As I have already implied, the philosophic vein that they have most consistently exploited is the esthetics of artistic creation, the philosophy of composition. Whether it be in an essay, a Horatian-style *art poétique* or within the confines of a concrete, self-regarding text, a French poet typically will explore those facets of poetic composition or artistic creation that interest him. Valéry, for example, was a theorist, an analyst, early and late, and his lifelong meditation on some of the most fundamental problems of art knew no generic boundaries. This is perhaps the deeper significance of the following observation by Jean Hytier: "Dès le début de sa production poétique, Valéry a doublé celle-ci de réflexions théoriques."[2] By the same token, even his most "philosophic" poems have a remarkably sensuous, incantatory quality. With Valéry, as James R. Lawler has pointed out, "the twin poles of

irony and incantation, detached statement and magical spell
. . . match the constant and complementary moods of reason
and mysticism, thought and feeling."[3]

No such integration of rhapsody and reflection can be found
in Guillaume Apollinaire, the poetic adventurer *par excellence* of
this century's first two decades. An extraordinary openness to
life, love and "l'esprit nouveau" in literature and the plastic
arts prevented the author of *Alcools* (1913) from engaging in
any sustained examination of his own continually evolving
practice, poetry generally or, Cubism and the Cubists aside,
broader questions of artistic creation and esthetic value. Apol-
linaire wrote a great deal, in the form of articles, prefaces and
notes, on his painter friends and acquaintances, but with a few
possible exceptions his poems can hardly be construed as medi-
tations on art, poetry or the creative process à la Valéry. Thus
in Apollinaire a rather well-defined line of demarcation sepa-
rates the creative from the critical intelligence. Also, his seem-
ingly inexhaustible enthusiasm for what was new in the world
around him presumably overwhelmed any impulse he may
have felt to stand back from his life, as it were, in order to
conduct an esthetic *examen de conscience*.

Yet Apollinaire was aware of and concerned about the kind
of poet he was. He expressed his feelings on the matter most
poignantly in "La Jolie Rousse," the poem which closes *Calli-
grammes* (1918) and which is considered his testament:

Soyez indulgents quand vous nous comparez
A ceux qui furent la perfection de l'ordre
Nous qui quêtons partout l'aventure[4]

Apollinaire thus saw himself as an exponent of adventure as
opposed to order. Given his passionate involvement with
avant-garde painting and sculpture, his Futurist manifesto, his
"Cubist" poems (such as "Zone") and the daring formal ex-
perimentation of *Calligrammes*, his was without question a pro-
foundly innovative spirit, especially as regards the syntax and

the visual-graphics of poetry. In certain respects, however, Apollinaire was quite traditional. The very form of *Le Bestiaire* (1911), the elegiac strain that runs throughout his work, his treatment of love and the beloved, the role he assigns memory, his use of seasonal (especially autumnal) imagery, all place him on the side of "tradition" rather than "invention," two terms he uses elsewhere in "La Jolie Rousse" as synonyms for order and adventure. Nevertheless, Apollinaire too, not unlike Valéry, sought to reconcile heart and mind. Further on in his poem-testament we read:

> O Soleil c'est le temps de la Raison ardente
> > Et j'attends
> Pour la suivre toujours la forme noble et douce
> Qu'elle prend afin que je l'aime seulement   (p. 314)

Thus his penchant for experimentation, for intuitive questing, is perhaps less compulsive and unreflected than is generally supposed, for he too dreamed of fusing system and spontaneity, method and adventure, in "la Raison ardente."

Apollinaire came closest to achieving his ideal of "la Raison ardente" in *Méditations esthétiques: les peintres cubistes* (1913). While he produced little or no poetry of a perceptibly speculative or analytical cast, he did write this small book of art criticism in which he reacted *as a poet* to what Picasso, Braque and others were accomplishing in the domain of painting. LeRoy Breunig and Jean-Claude Chevalier have lauded Apollinaire's marriage of poetry and art criticism as follows:

> . . . l'originalité d'Apollinaire est d'avoir étendu le domaine de la poésie moderne à la prose de la critique d'art en unissant ce que Baudelaire avant lui, dans les écrits des *Curiosités esthétiques* et de *L'Art romantique* d'une part, et dans *Les Fleurs du mal* de l'autre, avait maintenu nettement distinct. Apollinaire a inauguré ainsi pour le XXe siècle le genre de la "poésie critique." . . .[5]

The specifically hybrid nature of *poésie critique* reflects not only Apollinaire's dream of a "burning Reason" but also French poetry's age-old, unique blend of song and idea, lucidity and possession. The proliferation of this new form of writing since Apollinaire and the rise of Cubism suggests, among other things, that today even more than in the past French poets are seeking to combine sober analysis with flights of the imagination, whether consciously or not. The title of Pierre Reverdy's essay in *poésie critique* on Braque, "Une Aventure méthodique,"[6] captures this animating ideal perfectly. French poets have traditionally approached their work as a kind of methodical adventure, as at once a self-conscious experiment and an open-ended experience, but never has this central, Janus-like feature of French poetry been so salient as in the twentieth century, nor have the methodical adventurers been so diverse as they are in our time.

Though tremendously varied among themselves, the methodical adventurers of twentieth-century France nonetheless fall into two major classes, those for whom poetry is a means and those for whom it is an end in itself. In a broad sense these categories correspond to the two poetic traditions which over forty years ago Marcel Raymond, in *De Baudelaire au surréalisme*, traced back to Baudelaire, the tradition of poet-magus, the seer, and that of the self-absorbed artist.[7] Mallarmé and Valéry in particular exemplify the latter tradition for Raymond, while Rimbaud and Apollinaire, among others, represent the former. This thesis, which is in fact a brilliant insight into French poetry since Baudelaire, has contributed enormously to present-day understanding of this poetry. Nevertheless, Raymond's classifications, especially when abstracted from his nuanced, richly illustrated argument, tend to suggest polarization between *artiste* and *voyant* instead of dynamic polarity, uncompromising opposition rather than the ceaseless interplay within the same poet of contradictory but mutually supportive aims and impulses. The seminal strength of Raymond's book derives from the fact that at a very early date it stressed the central importance for modern French poetry of these poles, the poet as detached self-contemplator, impersonal Narcissus, and the poet as prophet, unveiler of the unknown.

In the years since Raymond's classic study first appeared, the debate, if it can be called that, between, on the one hand, the self-conscious makers and, on the other, the gifted visionaries, seems more and more to revolve around the status and function of language, or, more precisely, writing. Is language, or writing, the medium through which the poet accedes, if only fleetingly, to an absolute such as truth, being or the real, or is it the very domain he explores and exploits in order to create self-contained linguistic structures? In his recent study *Modern Poetry and the Idea of Language*, Gerald L. Bruns has provided terms and definitions that render this difficult basic question amenable to discussion and that properly emphasize the role of language in poetry.[8] Bruns proposes two headings under which poetry in general, but especially modern poetry, may be subsumed, the Orphic and the hermetic. "Hermetic poetry," he writes, "is intelligible only in terms of the work; it is not a 'saying,' not a predication or reference or disclosure; it is primarily a 'making'—the making of a closed structure of relationships among the components of a language" (p. 255). Orphic poetry, by contrast, is precisely a saying, a predication, a reference or a disclosure. It is named "after Orpheus, the primordial singer whose sphere of activity is governed by a mythical or ideal unity of word and being, and whose power extends therefore beyond the formation of a work toward the creation of the world" (p. 1). "The Orpheus myth," Bruns further observes, assumes "the power of the word to call up the world into the presence of man" (p. 6).

Despite their antithetical, even mutually exclusive orientations, both conceptions of poetry, as Bruns also points out, assert the primacy of language (p. 2). But to the extent that

Bruns's categories apply to twentieth-century France, the primacy of language for Orphic and hermetic poets is only one of several important points of contact between the two types. Both, for example, continue the progressive purification of poetry that began with Baudelaire, a process of ascesis whose goal has been to strip from poetry all that is non-poetic, such as conventional prosody, narrative development and moral or ideological concerns, so as to get at "la poésie pure."[9] Also, both Orphic and hermetic poets confer autonomy on the poem. To the former, the finished poem becomes a part rather than a reflection of the world, while for the latter it is suspended in a void like the world, which it annihilates. Finally, both conceptions of poetry adopt a fundamentally anti-Romantic stance, for each in its own way displaces the imperial self that informs so much nineteenth-century literature, a self that devours or invades the world. Among Orphic poets, the poet's self is often caught disintegrating; it is impinged upon, decentered, invaded by the world. For the hermetics, scarcely any self at all, other than that of the reader, transcends the grammatical subject of the discourse.

But it is perhaps in regard to just this point, the disappearance of the self in modern literature, that the abyss separating the means-oriented Orphic poets from the end-oriented hermetic poets comes into full view. As Paul de Man has noted, for a number of contemporary scholars and critics of poetry "a loss of the representational function of poetry . . . goes parallel with the loss of a sense of selfhood."[10] From this coupling of losses it follows that the distinction to be made between the splintered self of Orphic poets like the later Apollinaire and the absent self of hermetic poets (or *scripteurs*) such as those associated with *Tel Quel*, is not one of degree but rather one of kind. In their rigorously allegorical or contextualist posture, the *telquelistes* reject the notion that a poem expresses some pre-existing reality, or some aspect of the poet's self; for Ponge and Pleynet the reader's self alone structures the text. On the other hand, while the Orphic poet's self is fragmented and seized only in bits and pieces of perception jotted down serially, a self is still felt to be present, even as it is in the process of imploding. And however threatened, undermined or diminished this self may be, it validates and is in turn validated by a translinguistic reality.

Using the paired loss of self and referentiality in poetry as a touchstone, one can posit a sequential and possibly a genetic relationship between the Orphic and the hermetic poets of twentieth-century France. Both Ponge and Pleynet identify Lautréamont and his era (circa 1870) as constituting a definitive rupture with poetry's past, the end of referentiality in literary language and the beginning of an era in which reader supplants or merges with scriptor to become the text's structuring consciousness. And they see themselves advancing in Lautréamont's wake, continuing his work.[11] It is conceivable, however, that events nearer in time to Ponge's debut as a writer during the 1920's paved the way for him. Specifically, the Cubist experiments in painting and poetry in 1910-1920 appear a particularly likely milestone in the development of metapoetry, Ponge's own form of hermetic poetry. Paul de Man has persuasively argued that a poet as late in the day and as textually introverted as Mallarmé seems to have remained a representational poet and a poet of the self throughout his life.[12] The definitive loss of the self with the attendant disappearance of the mimetic in poetry probably came after Lautréamont and Mallarmé, not with them, however correctly they may be viewed as harbingers of this great change. The daring notational style of the later Apollinaire and of Reverdy's verse poetry of 1916-1918 (a radicalization of Rimbaud's style), redolent with intimations of a fractured if not yet completely eradicated sense of self, anticipates the tentative, fragmentary, persona-less writing of Ponge and Pleynet more directly than does anything one finds in Lautréamont.

Still, there is no continuum here; a missing link breaks the developmental chain. If literary Cubism points toward meta-poetry, in the end a gulf separates the two modes, the question of whether the poet founds, *inscribes*, a world of words with his writings or simply records, *transcribes*, in his poetry the evanescent drama of a consciousness that is imbedded in the world lying beyond words. Literary Cubism predates and even prefigures Ponge's earliest metapoetic efforts, but Apollinaire and Reverdy ultimately treat poetry as a means whereas Ponge and Pleynet consider poetry, i.e., the production of texts, *l'écriture*, an end in itself.

If anything, the gap between these two conceptions of poetry seems to have grown wider or to have become more formalized in recent years. To appreciate this phenomenon one has only to reflect upon the fate of French poetry over the last decade and a half. With the demise of *Mercure de France* and *Cahiers du Sud* in the mid-1960's, two extremely important outlets for poetry disappeared from the French scene. A more severe if more diffuse blow against poetry was struck in the last decade when criticism pushed its way toward the top of the literary hierarchy, and henceforth, it seemed, poetry would lag further than ever behind the other genres in popularity among the cultivated reading public. But in the years since 1960 the greatest enemy of poetry, of Orphic poetry in particular, has been something both vaguer and more pervasive than the emergence of criticism as a—if not the—major literary genre. Since that time there has been a growing tendency on the part of writers, especially those associated with the review *Tel Quel*, founded in 1960, to ignore traditional genre distinctions and, moreover, to view all writing as *l'écriture*, as an essentially self-justifying, autotelic activity, and not so much any longer as simply the means by which a work of art is created to take its place in the world or contact with some transcendent reality is sought. It was thus all the more remarkable that in the spring of 1967 a deluxe, high-quality magazine of mainly poetry was born. Without question this review, named *L'Ephémère*, was founded in part at least to fill the void left by the departure of *Mercure de France* and *Cahiers du Sud*. It seems equally clear that *L'Ephémère* was launched in reaction to the new literary ethos, epitomized by the *Tel Quel* group, which denied poetry the privileged status it had so long enjoyed.

During the five years of its existence (1967-1972), *L'Ephémère* opposed and complemented *Tel Quel* in a number of ways. For example, it is possible and even appropriate to consider certain figures who have been associated with *Tel Quel*, notably Francis Ponge, Marcelin Pleynet and Denis Roche, as representing one of the two main currents in contemporary French poetry. Similarly, Yves Bonnefoy, André du Bouchet and Jacques Dupin, editors of and frequent contributors to *L'Ephémère*, may be seen, together with their review (and its apparent successor, *Argile*, founded in 1973), as exemplifying the other principal direction in which the most advanced French poetry seems to be moving today. The poets of *L'Ephémère* belong to the tradition which cherishes close ties with and inspiration from the plastic arts, encourages formal innovation, views metaphor as the essential *res poetica*, tends to employ (in one way or another) the ordering device of a poetic persona and holds that poetry is a quasi-religious or Gnostic quest for knowledge of such absolutes as the sacred or being or, in A. Kibédi-Varga's words, "le réel universel."[13] Poetry in this perspective is thus a means, not an end in itself. Nor, as Bonnefoy has remarked in an essay on Du Bouchet, does poetry either begin or end in language.[14] The *Tel Quel* poets, on the other hand, believe that language, or writing, *l'écriture*, is virtually all there is and moreover that any absolute beyond language, such as being, is a chimera, whatever form the "text" (a term they prefer to "poem") may take.

L'Ephémère has another feature that underscores its opposition to *Tel Quel*. The cover of all twenty numbers of the review carries a reproduction of the same fading, emaciated Giacometti nude. Also, *L'Ephémère*, No. 1, is virtually a homage issue to Giacometti (as are, to a lesser degree, Nos. 8 and 18).[15] Finally, two of the editorial board members of *L'Ephé-mère*, André du Bouchet and Jacques Dupin, have each written several long studies on Giacometti.[16] All of this suggests that Alberto Giacometti (1901-1966), perhaps the most stub-bornly figurative artist of his generation, functioned as a kind of patron saint for *L'Ephémère* and its poets. If we compare, on the one hand, how Du Bouchet and Dupin view their "patron saint" with, on the other, what has been written about him by the "elder statesman" of *Tel Quel*, as Francis Ponge has been called,[17] we can see in still another way how the two reviews, and the two avant-garde currents that they reflect, differ.

Ponge is fascinated by Giacometti. At first blush this is sur-prising since in *Proêmes* Ponge is critical of Camus's "nostalgie d'absolu"[18] and, as Sartre has pointed out in reference to Giacometti, "l'unité merveilleuse de cette vie, c'est son in-transigeance dans la recherche de l'absolu."[19] But Ponge in ef-fect acknowledges the unlikely nature of his association with the Swiss artist when he characterizes the latter in relation to himself as "peut-être on ne peut plus différent."[20] Ponge stands out among Giacometti's many admirers because of his attitude toward what he considers the broader implications of the artist's work. Gazing upon the famous stick figures, he perceives in them with undisguised pleasure "le pathétique de l'exténuation à l'extrême de l'individu réduit à un fil."[21] He is gratified to speculate that after Giacometti "*on* sera près d'en avoir fini avec le *Je*."[22] The concluding section of his "Réflex-ions sur les statuettes, figures et peintures d'Alberto Giacometti" typifies Ponge's approach to the artist:

> C'est ce JE que vous avez réussi à faire tenir debout sur son jambage, sur son pied monstrueux, cher Alberto.
> Cette apparition mince et floue, qui figure en tête de la plupart de nos phrases. Ce fantôme impérieux.
> Merci!

Car grâce à vous, nous le tenons, ce pourceau de l'intelli-
gence, l'homme, ce sceptre, ce fil! notre dernier dieu.

Même sous le nom de PERSONNE, il ne pourra plus
nous crever les yeux.

Il ne s'agit que de prendre garde, et de surveiller son
agonie.[23]

Thus, contemplating Giacometti's ever shrinking figures,
Ponge is serene, detached and confirmed in his own belief that
an era is at last ending, an era whose values derived from a
sacrosanct regard for the individual and from the imperialism
of the ego. The "elder statesman" of *Tel Quel* looks at the "pa-
tron saint" of *L'Ephémère* with profound respect but without
sympathy, in the original sense of the word. Ponge simply
situates himself too far beyond Giacometti's dazzling record-
ing of Romanticism's final spasm to feel the pathos of that
effort.

In their writings on Giacometti, Du Bouchet and Dupin are
totally different in tone and point of view from Ponge. They
write about the artist out of an obvious feeling of kinship with
him and as if from inside his vision. Du Bouchet, for example,
observes in reference to Giacometti's sketches: "Rien de nous
sépare de la figure projetée qui surgira, et, tête ou montagne,
avant que l'esprit s'assure de son identité, se trouve logée,
comme une géode, au coeur du papier blanc."[24] In a somewhat
longer passage from "Giacometti, sculpteur et peintre,"
Dupin asserts:

Si nous nous risquons à franchir la distance prescrite, nous
voyons le personnage littéralement se défaire devant nos
yeux. . . . Vu de près, ce corps . . . n'est plus qu'une masse
déformée et crispée, boursouflée et atrocement distendue.
Nous assistons à son supplice et à sa disintégration. . . .
Nous participons à la dislocation de l'édifice humain par le
soulèvement, l'insurrection de la matière même dont il est
formé. Nous sommes impliqués dans cette ultime dégrada-
tion.[25]

The verb constructions in this passage betray the writer's involvement with his subject: *nous nous risquons, Nous assistons à, Nous participons à, Nous sommes impliqués*. How far we are here from Ponge's grateful but eerily removed approbation of Giacometti! Ponge celebrates in Giacometti what he reads as the evidence of contemporary man's failure to maintain the myth of individual existence as an arduous personal quest for spiritual reality. Du Bouchet and Dupin see a different truth in Giacometti. For them, all of the artist's figures, whether walking or falling, minuscule or elongated, are caught settling, disintegrating into their grounds via their monstrous feet. One moment more or but another step and they would slip away altogether. But that step not taken and that moment not yet come define the domain of the *L'Ephémère* poets and Giacometti, the ephemeral, collapsing situation of man, the human condition entropized.

Juxtaposing *Argile* (the apparent successor to *L'Ephémère*, as I have already noted) and *Tel Quel* throws into yet greater relief the differences between the two main currents within avant-garde twentieth-century French poetry. Launched in late 1973, and published (as was *L'Ephémère*) by Maeght, *Argile* is edited by the poet and art critic Claude Esteban, a former contributor to *L'Ephémère*. The publicity brochure for the inaugural issue of *Argile* carries what for all practical purposes may be considered the review's manifesto, a statement in which, though he never mentions *Tel Quel* by name, Esteban alludes not so indirectly to the beleaguered situation of poetry (that is, of a certain kind of poetry) in present-day France, a situation that *Tel Quel*'s mere existence helped to create. Esteban also sets forth in this manifesto the assumptions that undergird his (and *Argile*'s) conception of what poetry is. In recondite language that fairly bristles with Platonic, Pascalian and mystical overtones, he in effect claims for poetry the power to "convoquer l'obscur," to articulate "les raisons secrètes du coeur." Moreover, poets must search out, "une fois de plus, parmi les branches aveugles du multiple, l'orientation et la voie":

Entre les rhétoriques anguleuses et l'éperon intraitable
des idéologies, est-il place, aujourd'hui surtout, pour le
poème? Opiniâtres ou naïfs, nous le croyons encore, don-
nant pouvoir aux mots de convoquer l'obscur, d'inventer
au-dedans comme un souffle qui les traverse. Et telle pré-
sence soudain tangible, dans l'étoilement des idiomes et la
diaspora des contrées, vient confirmer, s'il était nécessaire,
les raisons secrètes du coeur.

Affronter l'étendue, l'erreur, la précarité de l'échange,
n'est point, tant s'en faut, s'y résoudre. Quelques chemins,
ici et là frayés, attestent l'espoir d'une concordance. Stèles
superbes ou signes à demi rompus sont là, moins pour nous
guider que pour exiger derechef une reconnaissance, un vi-
sage. A nous de les accueillir, à nous de tenter, une fois de
plus, parmi les branches aveugles du multiple, l'orientation
et la voie.

Ici, sans autre lieu que la terre vacante, la terre intacte
sous nos pas, et *dans l'incertitude où nous sommes*—disons-le
avec Reverdy—*de vivre si près du ciel sans jamais pouvoir le
toucher.*[26]

The manifesto's closing paragraph ("Ici, sans autre lieu . . .")
neutralizes somewhat the transcendental and idealist implica-
tions of the earlier paragraphs by stressing that no reachable
elsewhere exists, that there is only "la terre vacante, la terre
intacte sous nos pas." But the Reverdy quotation at the end
implies that man's lot is to live forever separated from that
to which he must forever aspire. In the final analysis, there-
fore, for Esteban and *Argile*, man's most urgent impulse, even
if it is foredoomed, is to leap "any where out of the world" (to
use Baudelaire's phrase). Thus, despite the absurdist coloration
of the last paragraph, the manifesto as a whole conceives of
poetry in a way that is not unlike the way in which at least one
distinguished contemporary theologian conceives of religion:
"Religion is the drive out of the self toward transcendence, the

thrust of man out of and beyond himself, out of and beyond the limited order under which he lives, in an attempt to open himself to the totality of existence and reach ultimate value."[27]

The quasi-religious thrust of *Argile*'s manifesto becomes even more evident when we compare this statment with "Joyce in Progress," the prefatory note to the special "Joyce" issue of *Tel Quel* that appeared in the summer of 1973, just six months before *Argile* made its debut:

> Le travail le plus important de la littérature du XXe siècle est encore, surtout en France, presque totalement méconnu. Plus de cinquante ans ont passé depuis la publication d'*Ulysse*. Trente-quatre, depuis celle de *Finnegans Wake*. Pourquoi ce silence bavard, anecdotique, somme errante de détails confus? Pourquoi cette réputation d'illisibilité ou de gratuité pour une oeuvre aussi claire (forme et sens)? Breton condamne Joyce sans l'avoir lu. Jung, de même. Et, de même, Miller. Résistance du spiritualisme occultiste et obscurantiste pour lequel, au fond, Joyce n'est pas un "bon fou" laissant place à un au-delà exploitable. Gênante, cette hyper-rationalité constructive. Inadmissible cette intégration-composition de la schizophrénie la plus déchaînée. Les cultes, les religions ont toujours la même posture: il leur faut un ailleurs dont le langage serait l'exposant. Or Joyce déplace en acte, en histoire, ce qui s'effectue de l'inconscient dans la langue. Et c'est tout un siècle de demi-lumières qui bafouille devant son éclairage-coupure, qui, donc, se dérobe, bouche, substantialise, psychologise, voulant sauver ses fétiches. Finalement sans succès: la cure suit son cours.[28]

The *Tel Quel* writers obviously see Joyce as the tidal wave of the future, the force that will ultimately swamp the "spiritualisme occultiste et obscurantiste" that Breton, Jung, Henry Miller and unnamed others represent. For Marcelin Pleynet and the other editors of *Tel Quel*, Joyce is the great "éclairage-coupure" who has proven once and for all that nothing transcends language but its own structure, especially its syntax, its combinatory powers, and that the structure of language and the structure of unconscious mind are one and the same thing. Significantly, Reverdy's "Notes sur la poésie," published (posthumously) in *Argile*, No. 2 (printemps 1974), offer a view of poetry that is diametrically opposed to the one espoused implicitly in "Joyce in Progress." For example:

> Grande poète celui qui sait capter dans son filet de mots la plus grande masse d'inexprimable. (p. 35)

> Petit poète celui qui met toute sa foi dans le pouvoir et dans la combinaison des mots. (p. 36)

The distance between *Argile* and *Tel Quel*, hence between the divergent conceptions of poetry that they embody, can also be measured in terms of their respective contributors, as well as in terms of the different "gods" (literary and other) they worship. Where *Tel Quel*, No. 54 (été 1973), contains texts by and about Joyce, *Argile*, No. 1 (hiver 1973), includes poems by Yeats (translated by Yves Bonnefoy). Where, as we have seen, André Breton, the "pope" of Surrealism, is disparaged by *Tel Quel*, *Argile*'s inaugural issue carries new poems by the former Surrealist René Char (pp. 6-24). Where one finds previously unpublished sketches by Braque in the first issue of *Argile* (pp. 25-32), Marcelin Pleynet, the editor of *Tel Quel*, praises Matisse and Mondrian at the specific expense of the Cubists.[29] Finally, where Wittgenstein eventually replaces Heidegger as a source of inspiration and epigraphs for Pleynet,[30] the first number of *Argile* opens with a poem by Heidegger (pp. 4-5). Together, these choices bespeak two internally consistent and mutually incompatible mind-sets, a metaphysical or spiritual orientation *versus* a concern with matters epistemological and linguistic, poetry as the way of beauty or truth, the "breath" of being, *versus* poetry (or writing) as the play and display of language in action, poetry as quest, search for the absolute, *versus* poetry as *fête*, celebration of the relative, of that which is at hand, words, poetry as means *versus* poetry as end in itself.

Among twentieth-century French poets certain figures stand out as particularly illustrative of this bifurcation of contemporary poetry into either a means-oriented or an end-oriented scriptural activity. Pierre Reverdy, René Char, André du Bouchet and Jacques Dupin, all dramatically and in their own distinctive ways, embody a conception of poetry that attributes to the poem the power to take us beyond the quotidian and the empirical to a realm of knowledge or value that is sometimes referred to as the Surreal, or at the very least the capacity to record for all time the nobility of such a search for transcendence, doomed from the start though it may be. Francis Ponge and Marcelin Pleynet, on the other hand, exemplify, with stunning force and clarity, a view of poetry, or writing, that would have us linger forever at just that juncture of experience and expression where words beget nothing but other words, and where the poem exists primarily in its relationship to other texts.

All of these poets, however, especially Reverdy, Ponge, Char and Dupin, come together in their common obsession with entropy, even if each one handles his obsession in a manner that befits both his specific nature as a writer and his status as either an Orphic or a hermetic poet. The thermodynamic phenomenon of entropy, which has been defined as "a drift toward an unstructured state of equilibrium that is total. . . . a leveling of energy until all distinctions are obliterated. . . . evolution in reverse,"[31] is evoked again and again in Reverdy by the imagery of collapse that permeates his poetry. In this sense Reverdy anticipates the "illumination" that Sartre's hero Roquentin experiences at the climax of *La Nausée*, Giacometti's entire production as an artist, and the vision of life that all but possesses Beckett, attaining its most "stoically comic" formulation (to paraphrase Hugh Kenner) near the end of *En attendant Godot* when Vladimir observes: "A cheval sur une tombe et une naissance difficile. Du fond du trou, rêveusement, le fossoyeur applique ses fers. On a le temps de vieillir. L'air est plein de nos cris."[32] Ponge for his part accepts the inevitability of cosmic decline, but locates this fate beyond the reach of our concern on the grounds that our actual experience of life (as opposed to any solipsistic reflection we may engage in upon it) involves us continuously in the birth, the rise into form, of awareness, of consciousness in the act of becoming. For Ponge, genesis, which is present and real, always prevails against merely projected entropy. As for Char, while he does not try to deny entropy, he seeks to transform it by an act of will into something positive, to turn the settling particles of pulverized life into a rising swarm, a tensed serenity and a shared suffering presence. Dupin, going a step further than Char, would absorb the final leveling of all and everything into his work and make destruction itself part and parcel of his poetic enterprise, whence his enormous admiration for Giacometti, who in his view has done precisely that.

These poets cluster together in other combinations as well. After Apollinaire, for example, all are deeply interested in the plastic arts, often in the same artist. (Ponge, Du Bouchet and Dupin, as I have indicated above, have written essays in *poésie critique* on Giacometti; Reverdy, Ponge and Char, on Braque; and Reverdy and Pleynet, on Matisse.)[33] All are true methodical adventurers, committed to incorporating into their art, at times directly, as such, the fruits of their analysis of that art. As remote from each other in era and in attitude toward writing as Reverdy and Pleynet are, both are devoted to exploring, albeit by diverse scriptural routes, the nature of metaphor. As divergent in their respective responses to Giacometti (with all that such a divergence implies) as Ponge and Dupin are, the latter's *Moraines* is closer in mode and intent to the former's *Proêmes* than it is to any other work. Bonds of admiration and emulation tie each of the three younger poets to one of the older figures: Du Bouchet has acknowledged the great impact Reverdy has had on him at a formative moment in his development,[34] while the influence of Char on Dupin, especially the Dupin of *Gravir*, and that of Ponge on Pleynet, for *Comme* in particular but also for the latter's interest in Lautréamont, are obvious even to the first-time reader of these poets. But what knits these poets together more tightly than anything else is the way in which each one of them sums up his era as a stage in the development of twentieth-century French poetry, and the way in which these stages, in turn, succeed one another to mark out, in retrospect, the two-pronged evolution of avant-garde poetry in France since 1910.

Avant-garde traditions or currents that are at once parallel and crosshatching assume concrete form in the work of Pierre Reverdy, Francis Ponge, René Char, André du Bouchet, Jacques Dupin and Marcelin Pleynet. By the middle of the 1910-1920 decade Reverdy was adapting for poetry many of the new esthetic values that were informing the canvases of his friends the Cubist painters. Also, in 1917-1918 he welcomed to the pages of his review *Nord-Sud* the earliest efforts of the future Surrealist triumvirate, Breton, Soupault and Aragon. Though a signer of the *Second manifeste du surréalisme*, Ponge reflects above all the crisis of faith in language which, according to Sartre, started to affect French intellectual life in the decade or so following World War I and to which Ponge's earliest writings bear eloquent witness.[35] Char, another signer of the *Second manifeste*, with his poetic production of the 1930's in particular, represents what is perhaps the high-water mark of Surrealism in poetry. Du Bouchet and Dupin demonstrate, among other things, the continuing vitality and the increasing centrality, during the post-World War II period, of what might loosely be called the Surrealist current in twentieth-century French poetry. Their review *L'Ephémère*, with its sumptuous design and solid material makeup, is anything but a typical ephemeral or "little" review. Numbering among its editors Michel Leiris, a frequent contributor to *La Révolution surréaliste* during the 1920's, *L'Ephémère* is more likely the final consecration of Surrealism, its ritual of passage into the mainstream of French poetry. Pleynet and the *Tel Quel* group as a whole, including in the present circumstances Ponge, threaten to subvert this tradition of "official" avant-garde poetry by casting writer and reader alike back to the surface of the poem, to its specific, local textuality. Paradoxically, Pleynet's relentlessly self-regarding stance as a writer links him to Valéry, the most "official" twentieth-century poet of them all. Thus today's "establishment" poetry, that appearing especially in *Argile*, has its origins in yesterday's avant-garde, while the anti- (or post-) Surrealist avant-garde of the *Tel Quel* group is rooted in an attitude toward poetry, or writing, whose prototypical exponent was admitted to the Académie Française a half-century ago. The following chapters focus on the six French poets of our time whose writings perhaps most faithfully reflect these avant-garde currents.

I. Pierre Reverdy

To situate Pierre Reverdy in the general picture of twentieth-century French poetry, one must examine his relationship to Symbolism, Cubism and Existentialism. Linking a single figure to all of these movements might perhaps seem inappropriate since to do so in effect runs together three distinct if slightly overlapping historical periods, as well as three quite different forms of human expression: poetry, painting and philosophy. Nevertheless, Reverdy's roots in Symbolism's ambience if not its esthetic, his formative encounter with Cubist art and theory and his early (and then recurrent) use of themes and images later to haunt Sartre and Camus, conspire, as it were, to structure his identity as a poet. Furthermore, in my view, it is precisely this conjunction of forces at work in his poetry that makes Reverdy an exemplary transitional figure between the "Banquet Years," as Roger Shattuck has aptly rechristened *la belle époque*, and our own era's bleak beginnings.

1. THE SYMBOLIST HERITAGE

By 1910, when at the age of twenty-one Reverdy arrived in Paris, Symbolism was in a moribund state as a source of poetic style and aspiration. Yet Guillaume Apollinaire and Max Jacob, the two poets who were to become Reverdy's literary mentors and who themselves must be classed among our century's most innovative writers, both bear Symbolism's impress on their work. This is particularly true of Apollinaire, whose in many ways revolutionary collection *Alcools*, published in 1913, exhibits not a few traces of Symbolist poetics—an overall elegiac tone reminiscent of Verlaine, a Baudelaire-like celebration of the redemptive powers of memory, Laforgue's notational style if not usually his irony and Mallarmé's skillful manipulation of harmonies and dissonances of sound and sense. Nevertheless, as Marie-Jeanne Durry and others have observed, already in *Alcools* Apollinaire was perfectly in tune with the 1910's, free of Symbolism's philosophical idealism with its attendant turning away from harsh reality and its implicit quest for unity. In Professor Durry's words, Apollinaire was "amoureux de la diversité, et des choses, . . . du multiple, du discontinu, de la surprise."[1] In short, aside from a continued reliance on narrative development in most of his verse, Apollinaire was by temperament more Cubist than Symbolist, and this turn of mind utterly transformed his literary origins.

Reverdy's debt to Symbolism is more problematic and hence harder to summarize than Apollinaire's. As I have already noted, Reverdy reached Paris too late to come under Symbolism's direct influence. Ostensibly, moreover, he rejected this influence. In March 1917, when the first issue of his review *Nord-Sud* appeared, it contained an anti-Symbolist manifesto, "Quand le symbolisme fut mort," written or at least signed by Paul Dermée, Reverdy's assistant on *Nord-Sud*.[2] Later Reverdy himself would speak of Symbolism's shortcomings in *Le Gant de crin* (1927).[3] Yet he greatly admired the three giants of the Symbolist era, Baudelaire, Rimbaud and Mallarmé, and more than once in his theoretical writings he contends that in art and literature one moves forward by building on the achievements of the past, not by ignoring them.[4] Also, although his theoretical writings are heavily indebted to the Cubist revolution in the plastic arts, Reverdy the theorist, not unlike Valéry, clearly aligns himself with the pure poetry tradition emanating from Baudelaire via Mallarmé.[5] Furthermore, his exaltation of art in *Nord-Sud* and elsewhere places him closer to Proust than to Max Jacob.

Reverdy's conception of the role of dream in creativity, which calls to mind not the relative passivity of the Surrealists' "récits de rêve" but rather Nerval's avowed desire to exploit the dream by directing it, points to what is probably the most important aspect of his debt to Symbolism. In language that anticipates Gaston Bachelard's notion of "la rêverie poétique," Reverdy affirms in 1924:

> Ce que j'appelle rêve d'ailleurs, ce n'est pas cette con-science totale ou partielle, cette sorte de coma que l'on a coutume de désigner par ce terme et où semblerait devoir se dissoudre, par moments la pensée.
>
> J'entends au contraire l'état où la conscience est portée à son plus haut degré de perception. . . .
>
> Le rêve du poète c'est l'immense filet aux mailles innom-brables qui drague sans espoir les eaux profondes à la re-cherche d'un problématique trésor.[6]

For Reverdy the poet's dream is thus an extremely receptive but not passive mode of consciousness, it is a harking to the inner self that never shades off into self-absorption. Somehow, the poet maintains a difficult, two-way vigilance that is indis-pensable to the creative act:

> Le poète est dans une position toujours difficile et souvent périlleuse, à l'intersection de deux plans au tranchant cruel-lement acéré, celui du rêve et celui de la réalité. (*Le Gant de crin*, p. 15)

Reverdy was in fact obsessed by the notion of a creative con-sciousness at once oneiric and actively engaged in the real world, a consciousness in which distinctions between self and other tend to blur without, miraculously, any loss to either. He is perhaps at his most lapidary on this matter in his 1923 essay on Picasso, where he asserts, with obvious admiration, that the artist "imagine d'après nature."[7] This apparent con-tradiction in terms (How does one *imagine* from nature?) gives us an insight into Reverdy himself, including his Symbolist lineage.

Over much of late nineteenth-century French poetry there hovers an atmosphere of dream. Thematically, moreover, the dream permeates this poetry. Guy Michaud, A. G. Lehmann and other students of French Symbolism have pointed out that the dream was the ideal state for the poet of this era to exploit and still remain insulated from an all too palpable and increasingly threatening outside world.[8] As early as Baudelaire, a perfect elsewhere exists in an imagination that has virtually severed its moorings in everyday, waking existence: "Là tout n'est qu'ordre et beauté/Luxe, calme et volupté." Not long after Baudelaire's death, Verlaine would both advocate and practice in his poetry vagueness, indirection, nuance, muted cries and the subtlest blends of melody and meaning. Mallarmé increasingly avoided the particular in his verse, preferring instead universalizing terms such as verbs in the infinitive form, abstract or functionally abstract nouns, few and generalizing adjectives, all set in poetry that is astonishingly dramatic by virtue of its endless internal antitheses but lacks the rough referential texture of, say, Lecomte de Lisle's earlier "Le Rêve du jaguar" or Apollinaire's later "Zone." All three Symbolist poets, Baudelaire, Verlaine and Mallarmé, flee the world of ordinary things, events and relationships for the imaginary, the idealized and the shimmer of words becoming poems. In this perspective, Impressionism in music and painting, that quintessence of artifice and delicacy, seems but an extension of Symbolism in poetry.

But just as Braque and Picasso step forward from the secure purchase of Cézanne's pictorial innovations and in the process literally pull Cubism out of Impressionism, Reverdy does not reject Symbolism but transcends it. He profits from its gains by tapping the polyvalent potential of words linked primarily to one another rather than to sharply delineated referents. At the same time, he discards the dreamy, nebulous quality of much Symbolist verse, and he plumbs the depths of his subjectivity without falling into solipsism. His poems, in his own words, are like so many "cristaux déposés après l'effervescent contact de l'esprit avec la réalité" (*Le Gant de crin*, p. 15).

There is in fact remarkable continuity between Reverdy's theory and his practice with regard to the dream. Paralleling his theoretical poetics, his working esthetic synthesizes dream-like, intermittent self-observation and the barest transcription of external phenomena. In its ensemble his poetry constitutes a kind of inventory of his outer and inner worlds. Yet thanks to Symbolism's lesson, his poetry is neither hard-edged in its fragments nor lacking in expressivity. Following Symbolism's example, Reverdy is totally concerned with bodying forth a highly subjective vision, but going beyond Symbolism, his vision is not in the slightest autistic, locked inside only his imagination. Rather, it is brought to expressive form in bits and pieces of perception that belong to the common storehouse of human experience. This fusing of inner and outer, of the private and the shared, gives Reverdy's poetry a pure, impersonal poignancy, a spare lyricism that one critic has dubbed "le lyrisme de la réalité."[9] The sustained self-auscultation of Symbolism cohabits in Reverdy with Cubism's steady gaze on the world outside.

A poem entitled "Le Soir," from *Les Ardoises du toit* (1918), illustrates, among other things, how important elements of the Symbolist heritage inform Reverdy's work:

Jour à jour ta vie est un immeuble qui s'élève
Des fenêtres fermées des fenêtres ouvertes
    Et la porte noire au milieu
Ce qui brille dans ta figure
               Les yeux
    Tristes les souvenirs glissent sur
    ta poitrine
Devant part vers en haut l'espoir
La douceur du repos qui revient chaque soir
Tu es assis devant la porte
  Tête inclinée
          Dans l'ombre qui s'étend
Le calme qui descend
Une prière
On ne voit pas les genoux de celui qui prie[10]

By its line-fragments "Le Soir" recalls the notational style of
Rimbaud and Laforgue, while the shifting left margin
suggests, in a general way, the Mallarmé of "Un Coup de dés."
The half-stifled, abortive theme of quest for some absolute, es-
pecially in the poem's last three lines, echoes French verse from
Baudelaire to Valéry. The title is nuance itself (evening being
neither day nor night but something in between), and it sets
the stage upon which a kind of *décadent* weariness can play it-
self out.

But the Symbolist residuum of "Le Soir" shows itself most
clearly by the manner in which details of observed reality,
while specific, are bathed in an atmosphere of daydream or
bemused wonder and, what is more telling, subordinated to
the exigencies of an unnamed but pressing malaise. A single,
mysterious hunger or need is adumbrated in a series of seem-
ingly discontinuous utterances. Together these utterances
form a cluster of explicit imagistic oppositions (rising/falling,
open/closed, light/shadow) that intertwine with a group of
implied thematic oppositions (hope/despair, security/anxiety,
faith/unbelief). These mutually reinforcing antitheses, rem-
iniscent of Mallarmé, revolve through the poem around the
gradual spread of darkness. The result, a spinning movement
within a descending one, that is, a downward spiral or vortex,
triggers indirectly, hence in true Symbolist fashion, a whole
complex of feeling, something akin to, even while exceeding,
quiet, agonizing desperation. The correlation between feeling
and form, between finely shaded emotion and delicately
wrought expression, seems perfect. Only a poet steeped in late
nineteenth-century French poetry could have written "Le
Soir."

2. LITERARY CUBISM

As is no doubt already obvious, it is difficult to speak about
the Symbolist aspect of Reverdy's poetry without at the same

time making reference to its Cubist dimension. The two are in fact inextricably related (as indeed are its Cubist and Existentialist components). Michel Décaudin, who in this respect typifies most historians of French Symbolism, maintains that philosophical idealism originating in Germany a century before constitutes a kind of common ideological backdrop for the otherwise heterogeneous poets of France's Symbolist period.[11] Ironically, however, it would seem that the essentially anti-Symbolist Cubist generation of poets, Apollinaire and Reverdy in particular, under the impact of advances made in the plastic arts by their friends Braque, Picasso and others, managed to assimilate and exploit Kantian idealist thought far more successfully than did their predecessors. In February 1912, the young critic Olivier Hourcade published an article in which probably for the first time in print the name of Kant was linked to Cubism. Specifically, Hourcade notes a parallel between, on the one hand, the Cubist painter's desire not to represent objects but rather to conceptualize them, and on the other, Kantian idealism.[12] In drawing this parallel, Hourcade makes an implicit but crucial distinction between representational art and non-representational art, between two painterly goals which Apollinaire a few months later would term, respectively, "la réalité de vision" and "la réalité de conception."[13] More recently, Gérard Bertrand has noted a similar distinction in Reverdy's theoretical pronouncements between "réalités visibles" and the "réel, dans ce qu'il a de permanent et de général." Of particular interest in the present circumstances is the fact that Bertrand couches the appeal Cubism held for Reverdy in philosophical terms and that he identifies the lesson Cubism offered Reverdy as that of a safe passage between the Scylla of descriptive poetry and the Charybdis of Symbolism:

> Pour Reverdy, le Cubisme représente la tentative la plus audacieuse d'une appréhension, par les moyens de l'art, des

réalités essentielles du monde. Instaurant un nouveau type de connaissance, le Cubisme devient un modèle pour la poésie: il lui enseigne comment concilier sa légitime aspiration vers le monde des essences avec le souci constant de ne pas se séparer définitivement du réel, il lui permet d'éviter le double écueil de la poésie descriptive et du symbolisme.[14]

What is most significant here is that Hourcade, Apollinaire and Reverdy (via Bertrand's paraphrase) are alluding to the technique of conceptualization, one of Cubism's most important contributions to the ongoing evolution of painting.

Reverdy was an intimate of the major Cubist artists throughout his sixteen years in Paris, 1910-1926. From 1912 onward, moreover, he was one of their most articulate defenders and explicators. Thus he was ideally situated to absorb some of the tenets of painterly Cubism into his own literary esthetic, and in a sense was encouraged to do so by Apollinaire's example. During his first eight years in the capital, Reverdy witnessed at close range and was profoundly impressed by Apollinaire's multifarious avant-garde activities. In 1912-1914, Apollinaire and several of his friends edited a magazine called *Les Soirées de Paris*. It was here that Apollinaire first published sections of *Méditations esthétiques: les peintres cubistes*, as well as "Zone," his longest "Cubist" poem and his first poem without punctuation, a device Reverdy was to employ in all of his verse poetry. The outbreak of World War I in August 1914 put an abrupt end to the "heroic" period of Cubism. Apollinaire died (of complications from a war injury) two days before the Armistice in 1918, but well before his death he had urged Reverdy to found another Cubist-oriented review, one that would continue the work of *Les Soirées*. Reverdy was only too happy to accede to his mentor's wishes, and on March 15, 1917, he brought out the first issue of *Nord-Sud*, the one review of the 1910-1920 decade which, even more readily than *Les Soirées de Paris*, might conceivably be thought of as the "official" organ of literary Cubism.

Nord-Sud, No. 1, is a central document in the development of literary Cubism. Its first three items are a brief homage to Apollinaire, Dermée's anti-Symbolist manifesto and Reverdy's essay "Sur le cubisme."[15] The second two items form the heart of the issue. Reading both essays in a single sitting, one is struck by the significant amount of similarity, even overlap, between them. Together, they suggest that for Reverdy and the *Nord-Sud* group, as far as ideological assumptions are concerned, there is no fundamental distinction to be made between painting and poetry. As Reverdy makes plain in "Sur le cubisme" and elsewhere in his theoretical writings, he particularly admires the Cubist painters because of their non-mimetic stance vis-à-vis nature. They do not try to copy or imitate nature, but seek instead to add to it with their works. Their paintings, consequently, are autonomous, that is, they have no slavishly dependent relationship to nature. A Cubist painting is a synthesis of many elements which the artist has refined from the raw materials that nature offers him. In Reverdy's words, as we have seen, Picasso does not paint from nature, he imagines from nature. With the goal of imitation done away with, perspective, the means traditionally employed to achieve that goal, is dropped. What folly anyway to attempt to create the illusion of three dimensions on the two-dimensional plane of the canvas. What disappears in the process is, of course, the traditional subject of the painting. To paraphrase Wylie Sypher, the "figure" in the Cubist painting has disappeared into the "ground" of the painting. A leveling process has occurred. No one element has an independent or superior role. The canvas is an ensemble or a structure of equal and interdependent elements.

If the Cubist painter rejects traditional perspective with its single point of view and its illusion of depth, he seeks to paint a non-imitative, non-decorative canvas. According to Reverdy (following Hourcade and Apollinaire), one of the chief means that the Cubist painter employs in his effort to create such a work is the technique of conceptualization, a process which, in

Reverdy's opinion, constitutes as important an advance in the evolution of painting as the invention of perspective was in the Renaissance. The Cubist painter takes from an object its principle "conceptualizable" characteristic—such as "la forme ronde d'un verre," notes Reverdy in "Sur le cubisme"—and he discards the object's other, ephemeral aspects. He "constructs" paintings in which objects become elements of the created work, their appearance as objects and logical relationships among them as objects remaining "outside" the work. Nor does the Cubist painter restrict himself to a single angle of vision; his point of view on the object of his attention can be multiple, to such an extent that he sometimes even dissects the object so as to see it from within, as it were.

How does the foregoing relate to poetry? For Reverdy (and one can find traces of this line of thought in Apollinaire as well), the demise of representational art corresponds to the demise of the anecdotal skeleton of the poem. The Cubist painter and poet, while eschewing a representational esthetic, assume nonetheless a fundamentally referential stance vis-à-vis material reality. In the words of Gérard Bertrand: "De même que ses amis peintres ne se sont jamais totalement affranchis des réalités visibles, de même Reverdy ne veut pas d'une poésie coupée de toute référence au réel."[16] But just as the Cubist painter is no longer willing to "copy" a subject as faithfully as he can while remaining in a fixed position, Reverdy in his theoretical writings opposes simply telling a story, describing a scene, or expressing an emotion by moving from a beginning through a series of stages to an end. He says at one point in Nord-Sud, "Affirmons d'abord qu'écrire n'est pas forcément raconter."[17] If the Cubist painting is non-imitative, the poem should be non-discursive and non-teleological. In both cases elements which originate in reality must be taken out of reality—by means of the conceptualization process—and simply juxtaposed in the painting or the poem. In former times one-point perspective had provided the painting with a mode of transition between foreground and background, between subject and setting, while discursive logic, traditional syntax and neatly modulated thematic development had provided comparable links or transitions in poetry. Now we are to see instead fragments on a canvas or on a page.

This brings us to Reverdy's theory of the image, first expounded in *Nord-Sud*, No. 13 (March 1918). For Reverdy, the image is not a simile, nor is it a metaphor if by metaphor is meant an implied analogy in which one of the two compared terms is functionally inferior to the other (as is the case, for example, with I. A. Richards' famous distinction between "tenor" and "vehicle"). Rather, the image for Reverdy is the bringing together of two equally important objects of attention not normally associated with each other, a rapprochement that sets off the spark of esthetic response in the reader. Thus, the various fragments of the Cubist poem, the bits and pieces of perception inscribed seemingly at random across the page, should, in theory at least, generate by their reciprocal action a whole series of sparks, of fleeting illuminations.

It is of course difficult to determine the precise amount of continuity that may exist between Reverdy's theory and his practice concerning the matter of Cubism, but certain attitudes and values inherent in Cubist art and theory, discussed by Reverdy in his notes and essays, quite obviously affect his poetry. We find, for example, in nearly all of his work of the 1915-1930 period, but especially in his verse poetry of that decade and a half, that perceptual consciousness would appear to take precedence over reflexive consciousness. Particularly illuminating in this regard is the epigraph to *Le Gant de crin*, Reverdy's 1927 volume of notes on art, man, God: "Je ne pense pas, je note." This guiding declaration (which should not be construed as an endorsement of automatic writing, which Reverdy opposed), has the effect of attributing value to the act of jotting down, of writing, at the specific expense of the processes of reflection, of Cartesian rationalism. It further suggests that the notational style of Reverdy's poetry is perhaps not merely a technique but a self-generating method and its own end, that we may well be dealing here with an incipient adept of *l'écriture* long before that term was to acquire its present-day application.

In Reverdy's poetry, sensations, fleeting memories and imaginings, quick associations and half-thoughts are simply recorded as such, or so it would seem, without any organizing personality to pattern them and make them meaningful. Any poetic voice or persona in Reverdy is so thoroughly merged with what it to all appearances only fitfully apprehends, that the very existence of a delimited, ordering subjectivity is called into question. The viewpoint of the Cubist painter breaks up into many viewpoints, while the subject of his painting sinks back or melts, as in a mosaic, into its setting. Similarly, the speaker in a Reverdy poem seems fractured, both multiple by reasons of the ever-changing personal pronouns and splintered into shards of incomplete, enigmatic utterances.

Implicit in all of this is a post-Cartesian world view, coupled with a fundamental anti-Romanticism. The Cubist still life, with the human figure significantly absent and with the illusion of pictorial depth scarcely attempted, finds its counterpart in Reverdy's apparently persona-less, non-anecdotal verse. If the former may be viewed as rejecting, among other things, the man-centeredness and the Classical norm for the human figure of post-Renaissance art, the latter would appear to undermine both Romanticism's egocentrism and Descartes' dualism. Also, the Cubist artist, whether poet or painter, creates by externalizing the content of his world-filled consciousness, his *Erlebnis*. How far are we here from Heidegger's idea of man as *Dasein*, as Being-in-the-world, or from Husserl's notion of intentionality, in which consciousness never exists as an independent *cogito* but always as consciousness of something, as forever "out there"? With Descartes, as

William Barrett observes, "man is locked up in his own ego," while for Heidegger "man does not look out upon an external world through windows, from the isolation of his ego: he is already out-of-doors."[18] Heidegger of course goes much further than either Reverdy or Picasso in exploding the subject-object dichotomy, but the Cubist generation of poets and painters may have been the first to sense that human consciousness has a dialectical structure, that the self or ego is but one term of a dyad.

According to J. Hillis Miller, the Romantic ego of nineteenth-century literature, imperial, devouring all outside itself, led inexorably to Nietzsche and nihilism. Nihilism, Miller further maintains, can be escaped only when "man turns himself inside-out and steps, as Wallace Stevens puts it, 'barefoot into reality.' " What Miller then goes on to say in reference to twentieth-century British and American poetry may also be applied, *mutatis mutandis*, to a development in twentieth-century French poetry that perhaps originates in Reverdy and Cubism:

> To walk barefoot into reality means abandoning the independence of the ego. Instead of making everything an object for the self, the mind must efface itself before reality, or plunge into the density of an exterior world, dispersing itself in a milieu which exceeds it and which it has not made. The effacement of the ego before reality means abandoning the will to power over things. . . . When man is willing to let things be then they appear in a space which is no longer that of an objective world opposed to the mind. In this new space the mind is dispersed everywhere in things and forms one with them.
>
> This new space is the realm of the twentieth-century poem.[19]

The poem "Drame," first published in the Cubist-oriented *Nord-Sud* and later reprinted in the Picasso-illustrated collection *Sources du vent*, contains a number of features which may be characterized as Cubist and which bespeak a post-Cartesian, anti-Romantic stance:

> Le rond qui s'agrandit
> > Est-ce la guillotine
> Réalité du film
> > mystère dans le crime
> Il passait à ton cou une corde plus fine
> Les yeux sont plus vivants
> > Ton âme est étalée
> Tu ne t'en doutais pas
> > c'est l'électricité
> Les traits en grossissant se sont presque effacés
> La passion fait remuer toutes les têtes de la salle
> > Mais dans l'obscurité
> où personne ne crie
> Un coup de pistolet qui ne fait pas de bruit
> Comment pourra-t-il sortir
> > Mystère acrobatique
> Le pouvoir surhumain du courant électrique
> > L'a fait partir
> Le policier déçu meurt devant la fenêtre[20]

Certain references in the text of "Drame" ("Réalité du film," "l'électricité," "toutes les têtes de la salle," "dans l'obscurité," "Un coup de pistolet qui ne fait pas de bruit") evoke a darkened theater during the showing of a silent movie. Other details in the poem suggest that the film in question belongs to the detective or mystery story genre ("la guillotine," "mystère dans le crime," "à ton cou une corde," "coup de pistolet," "le policier déçu meurt"). But is the drama referred to in the title unfolding on the screen? Not exclusively, we sense. It is perhaps also taking place in the hall, as well as within the soul of the spectator-persona, the poem's "tu." But that soul's drama is in turn spread over the screen ("Ton âme est étalée").

This centerless spectator-persona, silent, hidden in the dark, in fact seems to exist only in the silhouettes flashing before it, in the primal responses wafting across the hall that these flashes elicit from everyone in the audience ("La passion fait remuer toutes les têtes de la salle"), and in its own half-formed associations with these images and emotions. Does the spectator-persona, whose very existence as a discrete entity remains problematic at best, identify with the escaped (or simply off-camera) criminal? With the dying (or merely fading-out) detective? Perhaps with the aura of impotence and death that attends both these figures in conflict, a conflict we imagine on the basis of the text more than read about in the text.

The themes of impotence and death are introduced in the poem's first two line-fragments, which together form an unforgettable Reverdy-type image. (I shall return to this point below.) An implied contrast between feeble man and an overwhelming larger-than-life force runs through the poem. The presence of this force beyond man's power and ken is felt most directly in words and phrases such as "s'agrandit," "plus vivants," "en grossissant," "fait remuer," "pouvoir surhumain," "L'a fait partir." Like electricity, it lies outside men, but it reflects and perhaps even shapes his destiny ("Les yeux sont plus vivants/Ton âme est étalée"). It is both impenetrable and frightening (the two questions "Est-ce la guillotine" and "Comment pourra-t-il sortir" combined with the two mentions of "mystère"). Finally, it constitutes the second term of a lived discrepancy, the term of lethal experience that contradicts and ultimately destroys naive, unexamined expectation. Present, devastating lucidity is forever separated from past, reassuring bad faith: "Il pass*ait* à ton cou une corde plus fine; Tu ne t'en dout*ais* pas."

From the very beginning of the poem this overwhelming force is linked to death. Reverdy's opening image brings together the cone of light, small at the rear of the hall but instantly larger as it hurtles to the screen over the audience's heads, and the guillotine. The luminous beam and the instrument of death glimpsed for a split second in it are of equal importance to the thematics of the poem and thus occupy the same functional plane. Their tentative, fleeting juxtaposition here, moreover, is nothing short of stunning in its enriching appropriateness to the text, as well as in its originality. With these two line-fragments we have, as I have already indicated, a superb example of a Reverdy-type image, a true epiphany, dazzling, fugitive, born of the bringing together of two distant, never before juxtaposed, yet somehow related, realities. It is an image that seems a perfect realization of the poet's oracular definition, which begins: "L'image est une création pure de l'esprit. Elle ne peut naître d'une comparaison, mais du rapprochement de deux réalités plus ou moins éloignées. Plus les rapports des deux réalités seront lointaines et justes, plus l'image sera forte, plus elle aura de puissance émotive et de réalité poétique."[21]

Insofar as we can piece it together, the on-screen drama, quite literally a projection of what's occurring in *tu*'s soul, pits the detective against the criminal. Significantly, it is the detective who is dying in the last line, not the criminal, and he is expiring before a window, an object which since Mallarmé, whom Reverdy greatly admired, had come to symbolize as at once the opening that looks out upon the ideal *and* the eternal barrier, thwarted access, to the ideal (hence "policier *déçu*"). Man, that incurable detective, seeks truth, but he is doomed, because of the radical unfairness of life, never to find the answers he craves. Furthermore, he is cut down in his tracks by life, that arch criminal, that force which surpasses his own, intellectual and other, and which shows him no mercy. Reverdy's poem thus dramatizes the essential "scandale," in Camus' sense of that word, involved in living and dying.

In "Drame," the poet's self, through his surrogate the spectator-persona (who as *tu* is also the reader's and thus every man's surrogate), instead of being a unifying and hence con-

trolling center of consciousness in the grand Romantic man-
ner, is splattered across the screen, floating through the hall,
dominated and given whatever substance it has only by what it
apprehends. In the process, the subject-object dichotomy,
Descartes' dualism, has disintegrated. Just as "figure" is dis-
persed throughout "ground" in a Cubist painting, the poet's
mask in "Drame" is broken up into descriptive, narrative,
lyric and dramatic fragments. And there is no hierarchy among
the fragments; they function on a par with one another, and,
chronologically speaking, virtually co-exist, so little does
linear development structure them. If the Cubist artist re-
nounces perspective, the chief means of logical transition from
foreground to background in representational painting, in
"Drame" Reverdy abandons punctuation, standard syntax and
conventional visual-graphic form. He sacrifices normal articu-
lation (the counterpart in poetry of the modeling function of
chiaroscuro in painting?) in order to juxtapose heterogeneous
elements in collage or even montage fashion, and in this way
frees his poem from the bonds of discursive logic. In Auer-
bach's terms, Reverdy has opted for the Old Testament or
paratactic style over the Homeric or hypotactic style. The ref-
erential matrix specific to each line-fragment in "Drame" is
stripped away or at the very least drastically reduced, with the
result that each line-fragment's full expressive power is un-
leashed in the new context of the poem, of which it becomes a
constituent element. This process of purification would appear
to correspond to the Cubist painter's technique of conceptuali-
zation.

If "Drame" is unconventional in punctuation, syntax and
typographical disposition, in other respects it conforms to
readily recognizable formal conventions. Most of the nineteen
lines, for example, are metrically regular. There are eleven
hexasyllables (which in this case should also be considered
hemistiches), five alexandrines (complete with proper caesura)
and one tetrasyllable (line 18). When we convert the hexasyl-

lables into hemistiches and make the compressions in the text appropriate to that conversion, we find moreover that Reverdy exploits traditional rhyme and assonance to a considerable degree. Line 11 ("La passion fait remuer toutes les têtes de la salle") poses a problem in that it contains sixteen syllables. However, we soon realize that on the rhythmic level it is simply two octosyllabic verses side by side, since its final stressed syllable ("salle") breaks the poem's end-rhyme (or assonance) pattern while its eighth accented syllable ("remuer") maintains this scheme.

Line 15, "Comment pourra-t-il sortir," comprising seven syllables, is the only genuine deviation from the metric norm of the poem. Also, it is a deviation that would have been avoided had Reverdy simply written "peut-il" instead of "pourra-t-il," a change of tense involving, presumably, little or no change in meaning. Why, then, did Reverdy add the metrically jarring syllable? The lone seven-syllable line in "Drame," by its very unexpectedness, directs our attention, paradoxically, past the poem's appearance of formal randomness to its alexandrine foundation. And the more conscious we become of the conventionally rhythmic substructure of "Drame," the more we realize that Reverdy's notational technique has a formulaic base, that he relies heavily on metrical clichés, and perhaps lexical ones as well since his diction could hardly be more common. Looking closer at "Drame," we see that it is filled with what are in a sense formulae, that here, and no doubt elsewhere too, Reverdy manipulates ready-made phrases and received metric forms in the same way that the Cubist painter arranges on his canvas commonplace objects that have been conceptualized, conventionalized as geometric forms.

If line 15 by its sprung rhythm effectively lays bare the poem's traditional prosody, through its verb tense (future), mode of discourse (interrogative) and diction (stark and elemental), it adds a unique, indispensable component to the poem's thematics. For the phrase "pourra-t-il" not only interrupts the beat, it also contains the poem's only future, a tense that conveys the unchanging nature of the terms of the drama. Rather than "How can he get out?" we read "How will he (ever) be able to get out?" More directly than any other line in the poem, it suggests that the "Drame" referred to in the title is the experience of the absurd, the inalterable discrepancy (or "divorce" in Camus's parlance) between what we want and what we get, between what we seek and what we find.

As we have seen, Reverdy counters Descartes' "Je pense, donc je suis" with subverting parody: "Je ne pense pas, je note." Like some imaginary jongleur-scribe scribbling his performance-version of an epic, Reverdy in "Drame" and the rest of his *oeuvre* juggles endless permutations and combinations of a large but finite stock of hemistiches. He asserts in *Le Livre de mon bord*: "Le poète est un kaléidoscope. Il entre peu de chose dans l'infinie diversité de ses combinaisons."[22] Each round of juggling, moreover, each twist of the kaleidoscope transmits not some intended idea or feeling on Reverdy's part ("Je ne pense pas . . ."), but instead provokes a particular, complex emotion never experienced before by either poet or reader: "Il ne s'agit pas d'exprimer ou même de transmettre, comme dit Valéry, *un état poétique*—il s'agit de le provoquer," he notes in *En vrac*.[23] His creative method is perhaps best captured in the title of his long essay on Braque, "Une Aventure méthodique." Poetic composition is Reverdy's methodical adventure, dazzling improvisation, never automatism, is his style.

3. POET OF NAUSEA

The impact of Cubist esthetics on Reverdy's compositional or scriptural techniques might appear to place him among the hermetic poets of his day, and yet nothing could be further from the truth. For like that other juggler of formulae, the traditional oral epic singer, as a poet Reverdy serves not art but religion in its most basic sense. Poetry for him is a quasi-sacred means, not an end in itself: "La poésie, c'est le bouche-abîme du réel désiré qui manque."[24] His poems serve to unleash and then encapsulate both his own and his reader's anguish in the face of life's absurdity.

Long before Sartre's hero in *La Nausée*, Roquentin, was to speak of his illumination in terms of "affalements," "affaissements" and "écroulements," images of collapse and implosion were haunting Reverdy. With his characteristic self-knowledge as a poet, he once observed in a letter to Jean Rousselot: "Je crois qu'on n'a jamais vu, dans mes poèmes, que la terre n'a jamais été solide sous mes pieds—elle chavire, je la sens chavirer, sombrer, s'effondrer en moi-même."[25] Indeed, a convulsive drift, slide or descent lurks at the heart of virtually every one of his poems. As early as 1915, when he published his first collection, *Poèmes en prose*, Reverdy's entropic vision, his obsessive concern with the decline of form toward formlessness, is manifest. "Fétiche," in *Poèmes en prose*, is particularly significant as regards the meaning of this phenomenon for the poet:

> Petite poupée, marionnette porte-bonheur, elle se débat à ma fenêtre, au gré du vent. La pluie a mouillé sa robe, sa figure et ses mains qui déteignent. Elle a même perdu une jambe. Mais sa bague reste, et, avec elle, son pouvoir. L'hiver elle frappe à la vitre de son petit pied chaussé de bleu et danse, danse de joie, de froid pour réchauffer son coeur, son coeur de bois porte-bonheur. La nuit, elle lève ses bras suppliants vers les étoiles.[26]

Our initial impression, that of delicately wrought beauty or stylized motion, is quickly erased as we soon realize how much the verbs "se débat" and "danse" (twice) contribute to the poem's overall effect. Before very long, the doll becomes indistinguishable from its frantic and pathetic gestures and we are cast into a brooding meditation upon some of the more de-

pressing implications of the poem's title. We also sense early
on that the entire text derives tautologically from a binary op-
position that is implicit in the title, the self-contradictory no-
tion of powerless magic.

But what specifically in the text of "Fétiche" undermines
our day-to-day, expedient assumption that all is well? In the
very first sentence there are two indications of the doll's
helplessness, the verb "se débat" and the final phrase "au gré
du vent." Reverdy ends his second sentence with a device he
will employ throughout his life, the appended relative clause
that keeps everything already introduced unstable. Fur-
thermore, the words in question, "qui déteignent" (a near
homonym of "éteignent," one of Reverdy's favorite vocables),
tell us that the doll's hands, and perhaps her dress and face as
well, are in the process of losing their pigmentation, of fading
toward blankness. With the next short sentence—"Elle a
même perdu une jambe"—we learn that complete disintegra-
tion is already in progress. It is thus in a mutilated and decay-
ing condition that the doll performs her dance. Then comes
perhaps the most cruelly ironic statement in the whole poem:
"Mais sa bague reste, et, avec elle, son pouvoir." On one level,
this sentence simply counters the theme of decay. On another
level, however, it admits the ravages of time by zeroing in on a
mere remnant of the doll's former splendor, her ring, which is
now claimed to be the source of her power. But, we must ask
ourselves, is this claim really credible, imbedded as it is in the
middle of such a loss-dominated text? The phrase "son coeur"
and its expanded echo "son coeur de bois porte-bonheur" em-
phasize at once the brave and pitiable qualities of the doll, its
quintessential mortality. Moreover, repetition with negativiz-
ing expansion ("danse, danse de joie, de froid" and "son coeur,
son coeur de bois") works in concert with the disquieting
internal rhyme or homophony ("joie," "froid," "bois") to con-
taminate "bleu" retroactively (now become "bleu de froid")
and to select in advance one semantic element within

"suppliants," the sterile posture of supplication and not the answered prayer, the poignancy of an attitude, not its potency. The sudden enlargement of focus that closes the poem underscores the fetish's puniness and total lack of efficacy by projecting its bereft situation onto the cosmic plane.

A heart beats (a function that is extremely important in many other Reverdy poems), and a heart is the source of courage and tenderness. But a wooden heart has as much chance of beating and inspiring strong emotions as a one-legged dancer has of dancing her way to heaven. This doll is therefore especially doomed, for its magic is illusory, it has no power at all to stay the relentless erosion of the cosmos. Is the doll's lot but a caricature of our own? Doubtless it is, since to live is to die slowly but surely, whether gaily or in cold terror. Nothing will stop the "danse macabre" but the final collapse of all and everything.

"Fétiche" reminds us of Sartre's paradoxical description of man as a "passion inutile." Significantly, the two contradictory and mutually limiting forces, passion for life and the instinctive knowledge of the inefficacy of such passion, form the generating dialectic of Reverdy's entire *oeuvre*. In Reverdy's poetic universe, man's passion prevents his awareness from becoming paralyzing self-consciousness. At the same time, his alert state checks his passion's élan by revealing its uselessness. Tragically aware, he keeps moving along, one step at a time, one heartbeat at a time, falling by stages and in spite of himself under the crushing burden of existence. Clearly man's lot, according to Reverdy, is not unlike that of Sisyphus.

Appropriately, the blurred silhouette of the legendary Corinthian is glimpsed here and there throughout *Poèmes en prose*. Reverdy never mentions him by name, nor does he sketch the hero in straightforward fashion. Nevertheless, various aspects of Sisyphus's well-known punishment appear and reappear in this collection. The pertinent sentences in "L'Envers à l'endroit" are the most explicit and complete:

Il grimpe sans jamais s'arrêter, sans jamais se retourner et
personne que lui ne sait où il va.

Le poids qu'il traîne est lourd mais ses jambes sont libres
et il n'a pas d'oreilles. (*PT*, p. 54)

The essentials are here: the climbing figure, his single-
mindedness, the great weight that he drags, even the con-
tradictory notion that he is free and still not free ("ses jambes
sont libres et il n'a pas d'oreilles"). "La Saveur du réel," the
poem that follows "L'Envers à l'endroit," anticipates, in tele-
scoped fashion, Camus's view of Sisyphus's "enlightenment"
during his descent from the summit:

Dans sa chute il comprit qu'il était plus lourd que son rêve
et il aima, depuis, le poids qui l'avait fait tomber. (*PT*, p.
55)

The two poems converge on the notion of excessive weight that
is about to or is in the act of causing someone to fall.

In other poems the emphasis is placed on the related theme
of the long march. "Marche forcée" (a particularly apt title for
a Reverdy poem) ends with another partial prefiguration of
Camus's conception of Sisyphus:

Cependant, chaque jour qui te désespère te soutient. Mais
va, le mouvement, le mouvement et pour le repos ta
fatigue. (*PT*, p. 15)

In "A l'aube," where fatigue has already taken its toll, the legs
have given out and are now folded up (a common manifesta-
tion of collapse for Reverdy):

. . . les jambes repliées sous lui il marche sur ses ailes. . . .
(*PT*, p. 23)

Heaviness, struggle and fatigue, satellite themes of the long
march, are everywhere in *Poèmes en prose*.[27] Even more preva-
lent, and also belonging to the long march cluster, is the

theme of the interminable yet terminal series of rise-and-fall acts (footsteps, drum rolls, rising and falling itself, repeated or vivid yet progressively vanishing scenes).[28] Joining the theme of the long march to the theme of diminishing pulsations are terms such as "convoi," "caravane," "cortège" and (in other collections) "cavalcade," each of which connotes separate units in a bobbing procession relentlessly advancing into the distance. This connotation, moreover, is reinforced indirectly by Reverdy's assiduous avoidance of a word like "défilé," which would evoke the uniform, undifferentiated aspect of a marching group and thus alleviate the oppressive, Sisyphean tone of the poems.

There is no evidence that Reverdy had any impact on Camus, but their affinity is real enough and it is rooted in more than just a common fascination with the figure of Sisyphus. Indeed, in chapters other than the essay on the legend itself, *Le Mythe de Sisyphe* contains countless statements that virtually gloss *Poèmes en prose*. In one of his many definitions of the absurd Camus asserts:

> . . . s'apercevoir que le monde est "épais," entrevoir à quel point une pierre est étrangère, nous est irréductible, avec quelle intensité la nature, un paysage peut nous nier. . . . cette épaisseur et cette étrangeté du monde, c'est l'absurde.[29]

It is precisely the unexpected "thickness" or "foreignness" of the world that Reverdy renders in *Poèmes en prose* with two rather simple stylistic devices. In poem after poem an inordinate number of verbs are in the negative. There is also the noticeably high frequency of the words *plus, moins, si* (the intensifier), *autre* and *trop*, all of which, like *ne . . . pas*, express deviation from some projected norm. Both the negative and the emphatic *si* are found in "Toujours seul":

> Dans la rue où nos bras jettent un pont, personne n'a levé les yeux, et les maisons s'inclinent.

Quand les toits se touchent on n'ose plus parler. On a peur de tous les cris, les cheminées s'éteignent. Il fait si noir. (*PT*, p. 13)

The verbs *s'inclinent* and *s'éteignent* directly convey the beginning of implosion. Hence, while collapse is what is in fact (and in act) encountered, something else was anticipated—someone's raising his eyes, daring to continue talking, a night not quite so black. This discrepancy (or "divorce," in Camus's language) between expectation and experience is the absurd.

The malaise inspired by the awareness of this discrepancy provokes an unabashed cry of lamentation—which is indeed rare for Reverdy—in *Poèmes en prose*'s "Hiver":

O monde sans abri qui vas ce dur chemin et qui t'en moques, je ne te comprends pas. J'aime la tiédeur, le confort et la quiétude.

O monde qui les méprises, tu me fais peur! (*PT*, p. 14)

The verb "vas," which expresses the perpetually ongoing process of life, demolishes "quiétude," the state to which the poet ardently aspires. And the chasm that separates the dream of peace from the reality of flux produces "peur." Again a passage from *Le Mythe de Sisyphe* can shed light on a Reverdy poem:

Heidegger considère froidement la condition humaine et annonce que cette existence est humiliée. La seule réalité, c'est le "souci" dans toute l'échelle des êtres. Pour l'homme perdu dans le monde et ses divertissements, ce souci est une peur brève et fuyante. Mais que cette peur prenne conscience d'elle-même, et elle devient l'angoisse, climat perpétuel de l'homme lucide "dans lequel l'existence se retrouve." (p. 40)

The full significance of the fact that "Hiver" ends with the word "peur" is now evident. Unlike Heidegger and Camus, Reverdy does not go beyond his fear to *angoisse*, for though persistently aware of his fear, he is just as persistently unintellec-

tual in its regard. He neither closes his eyes to the absurd nor
does he try to evade his reaction of terror through the distanc-
ing effect of analysis. The components of his poems, in fact,
appear to be instances of the "peur brève et fuyante" that
Camus sees as Heidegger's unreflected "souci."

This "peur brève et fuyante" also haunts the hero of *La
Nausée*, inasmuch as Heidegger's "souci" and Roquentin's
"nausée" are but different perspectives (a philosopher's *versus* a
fictional protagonist's) on the same human response. We now
begin to suspect that existentialist nausea constitutes the very
stuff of Reverdy's poetry. And while there is nothing in Sartre
to suggest that he was influenced by Reverdy any more than
was Camus, the climax of *La Nausée*, the pages devoted to
Roquentin's "illumination" in the public garden, would seem
to confirm our suspicion that a significant overlap in world
views links the two writers. It will be recalled that when the
hero of *La Nausée* attempts to explain his sudden insight into
the nature of existence, certain expressions, ideas and images
occur repeatedly. Of these, the most common (and by now
surely the best known) is the phrase "de trop," with which
Roquentin seeks primarily to verbalize his feeling of alienation
in a hostile universe. Other notions that one usually associates
with the word "trop," such as excess and impingement, also
pervade the novel's climactic pages:

> Je ne le *voyais* pas simplement ce noir: la vue, c'est une in-
> vention abstraite, une idée nettoyée, simplifiée, une idée
> d'homme. Ce noir-là, présence amorphe et veule, débordait,
> de loin, la vue, l'odorat et le goût.[30]

The verb "déborder," the key word in the above citation, is a
verbal "trop" that plays a crucial role in this section of *La
Nausée*:

> En vain cherchais-je à *compter* les marronniers, à les *situer* par
> rapport à la Velléda, à comparer leur hauteur avec celle des

platanes: chacun d'eux s'échappait des relations où je cher-
chais à l'enfermer, s'isolait, débordait. (p. 163)

Against this background, puzzling sentences in Reverdy's
Poèmes en prose become perfectly clear: e.g., "Tout est inerte et
trop grand pour ses yeux et son coeur" ("Voyages trop grands,"
PT, p. 43). As in the case of Roquentin, the inert "too-
muchness" of everything, its definitive "otherness," exceeds
the observer's capacity to absorb, to understand, to control.

The most important similarity between Reverdy's vision
and Roquentin's, however, concerns an image that is implicit
in the very notion of "too-muchness." The words "trop" and
"déborder" suggest that some kind of explosion will soon be or
is actually taking place. We have already noted that the image
of collapse or implosion, explosion's underside, dominates Re-
verdy's poetry from the beginning. In the climax of *La Nausée*,
more than any other single element, the image of collapse
seems to sum up Roquentin's complex intuition into the na-
ture of existence:

> Dans un autre monde, les cercles, les airs de musique
> gardent leurs lignes pures et rigides. Mais l'existence est
> un fléchissement. (p. 162)

In Roquentin's new awareness, mythic Eros loses out to real
Thanatos. The trees in the public garden no longer symbolize
the sturdy robustness of unyielding growth, but represent in-
stead what they are in themselves, living organisms fated to
shrivel, perhaps even now, to a wrinkled, nondescript heap. In
the end, the "affalement" of a phallic fiasco is transformed into
a gelatinous "affalement" of cataclysmic proportions (pp.
169-71).

For Reverdy's part, his obsession with "affalement" and
with its supporting themes and images becomes even more ap-
parent in the collections that come after *Poèmes en prose*. The
tendency is already evident in *La Lucarne ovale*, which was pub-

lished just one year later in 1916. Two consecutive poems to-
ward the middle of this collection, "Ruine achevée" and "Pour
le moment" (*PT*, pp. 110-13), afford exceptionally revealing
insights into the poet's central preoccupation. The former
poem, for example, culminates in an image of collapse that
formulates, with an amazing economy of means, the desolate,
contingent, in-act quality of man's tragically absurd slouch
toward nothingness:

> Un pan de décor qui s'écroule
> Dans la nuit

Significantly, on one occasion in *Le Mythe de Sisyphe* (p. 27)
Camus uses the same image to suggest the absurd: "Il arrive
que les décors s'écroulent."

In the opening couplet of "Ruine achevée" the poet admits
frankly what he had merely hinted at in *Poèmes en prose*, that he
considers himself to be in a bereft state with respect to some
previous condition of wholeness or fuller capacity:

> J'ai perdu le secret qu'on m'avait donné
> Je ne sais plus rien faire

He then enumerates, with a rapid crescendo in pathos and hor-
rific mutilation, three figures who embody his desperately de-
prived plight:

> Un moment j'ai cru que ça pourrait aller
> Plus rien ne tient
> C'est un homme sans pied qui voudrait courir
> Une femme sans tête qui voudrait parler
> Un enfant qui n'a guère que ses yeux pour pleurer

Having projected himself thus into his fellow sufferers, the
poet remains outside himself long enough to review his life, to
hate it for its very aliveness, and finally to "rejoin himself"
empty-handed:

Pourtant je t'avais vu partir
Tu étais déjà loin
Une trompe sonnait
La foule criait
Et toi tu ne te retournais pas

Nous avons un long chemin à suivre pas à pas
Nous le ferons ensemble

Je déteste ton visage radieux
La main que tu ne tends
Et ton ventre tu es vieux
Tu me ressembles

Au retour je ne retrouve rien
On ne m'a rien donné
Tout est dépensé

We see in these four stanzas, in addition to the now familiar
theme of life as a long and arduous march ("Nous avons un
long chemin à suivre pas à pas"), an unequivocal expression of
disgust with life. At the end of a second enumeration, this one
progressively intimate ("Je déteste ton visage radieux/La main
que tu me tends/Et ton ventre . . ."), the poet is suddenly re-
pelled by his physical self and he ends the stanza abruptly with
a pitiless yet poignant double observation (". . . tu es vieux/Tu
me ressembles") that completes two subtly demoralizing
rhyme sequences: *ensemble/tends/ventre/ressembles* and *radieux/
vieux*. Between the lines "Tu me ressembles" and "Au retour je
ne retrouve rien" a wrenching return to self occurs. The next
two lines ("On ne m'a rien donné/Tout est dépensé") bring us
back to the beginning of the poem and the theme of loss,
privation and impotence. For the fourth time the annihilating
word "rien" is closely associated with either "je" or "me."
Thus, coming as it does at this point, the final couplet implies
personal tragedy despite its impersonal language, and, con-

versely, a particular case exemplifies a universal condition: "Un pan de décor qui s'écroule/Dans la nuit."

The poem that follows "Ruine achevée" would at first glance appear to belie it completely. Yet even this seemingly jubilant poem, entitled "Pour le moment," bears within itself the germ of its own denial; an ironic counterstatement courses beneath the façade of its cheerful language. While appearing to rhapsodize about a privileged moment, the poet in reality does just the opposite. Only "for the moment," he in effect tells us, can we delude ourselves into believing that "la vie est simple et gaie":

> La vie est simple et gaie
> Le soleil clair tinte avec un bruit doux
> Le son des cloches s'est calmé
> Ce matin la lumière traverse tout
> Ma tête est une rampe rallumée
> Et la chambre où j'habite est enfin éclairée
>
> Un seul rayon suffit
> Un seul éclat de rire
> Ma joie qui secoue la maison
> Retient ceux qui voudraient mourir
> Par les notes de sa chanson
>
> Je chante faux
> Ah que c'est drôle
> Ma bouche ouverte à tous les vents
> Lance partout des notes folles
> Qui sortent je ne sais comment
> Pour voler vers d'autres oreilles
>
> Entendez je ne suis pas fou
> Je ris au bas de l'escalier
> Devant la porte grande ouverte
> Dans le soleil éparpillé

Au mur parmi la vigne verte
Et mes bras sont tendus vers vous

C'est aujourd'hui que je vous aime

While the Pollyanna-like first line at once puts the reader familiar with Reverdy on his guard, two verses in the second stanza make it plain to any reader that something frenetic and doomed is going on. The lines in question, "Ma joie qui secoue la maison/Retient ceux qui voudraient mourir," subvert the poem's joy by accentuating its stolen, unreal quality; it dwells in a false moment of arrestation. The tension introduced here grows in the lines that follow—despite their Eluardian appearance—until it freezes the poet in a posture of taut, concentrated effort: "Et mes bras sont tendus vers vous." The last line is set off typographically from the rest of the poem just as the day in question stands like a statue outside time and is thus protected from its ebb. A lyric pyramid narrows to the vanishing point: "C'est aujourd'hui que je vous aime." How far we are from the radiant, all-embracing endings of Eluard's poems!

In the context of Reverdy's entire canon "Pour le moment" emerges as hardly even the exception of hope that proves the rule of despair. Its third line has particular relevance in this regard: "Le son des cloches s'est calmé." It tells us that the sound of the bells has ceased altogether, that stillness reigns supreme. But in Reverdy's poetic universe silence or peace comes only with death. This point is made with special force in a poem entitled, fittingly enough, "Son de cloche," which appeared in the 1918 collection *Les Ardoises du toit*:

Tout s'est éteint
Le vent passe en chantant
                    Et les arbres frissonnent
Les animaux sont morts
Il n'y a plus personne

Regarde
Les étoiles ont cessé de briller
        La terre ne tourne plus
Une tête s'est inclinée
        Les cheveux balayant la nuit
Le dernier clocher resté debout
        Sonne minuit (*PT*, p. 190)

Twelve uneven lines, twelve uneven peals of the bell; the "witching hour" is at hand. We are convinced by this poem that when the last echo of the tolling subsides, the last vestige of life itself will have been extinguished. Next to "Son de cloche," "Pour le moment" seems at best a harmless fantasy and at worst a cruel joke. When all sound ceases, no feeling of plenitude or love will inundate the poet, no magical escape into atemporal communion with the world will offer itself to him. The line "Le son des cloches s'est calmé" in fact portends doom and nothing else, as "Son de cloche," its gloss, shows. As would a dream, "Pour le moment" inflates and embellishes a split second during which the poet refuses his true vision, the vision he shares with Roquentin, that of life as active decomposition. The "quiétude" whose absence Reverdy had lamented in *Poèmes en prose*'s "Hiver" is no more present here than it was there.

"Pour le moment" demonstrates that the poet's *anti-destin* must lie in his facing up unflinchingly to the very cosmic erosion that this poem on the surface denies. Of course, no miracles are to be expected; the poet can no more exorcise his profound unquiet than he can throw off his human condition. Logically, his poems can only record his repeated failures at changing his *ennui* into *extase*. This is precisely what Reverdy's poems do. Thus, what Camus says about the creative artist in *Le Mythe de Sisyphe* applies particularly well to Reverdy: "La suite de ses oeuvres n'est qu'une collection d'échecs" (p. 153).[31] From *Poèmes en prose* in 1915 through the downward shift represented by *Ferraille* in 1937[32] to "Sable mouvant," written in 1959 during his last year of life,[33] Reverdy's texts do indeed constitute a "collection d'échecs," so many transcriptions of as many shattering encounters with the absurd. Not surprisingly, given his capacity for penetrating self-scrutiny, his lucidity in this matter is complete: "Tant aimer la vie et ne pouvoir l'étreindre—déchirer sa peau aux épines de son injustice et de son absurdité . . . la glorifier, la maudire—par l'art—voilà la cheville, l'anneau qui enchaîne et qui fait le poète. Exprimer cet échec, cette horrible défaite pour ne pas en mourir."[34]

This brings us to the question of Reverdy's profound appeal. He transfigures his experience of the absurd, the nausea or malaise that accompanies the fleeting awareness of the contingency of all things, by imparting to such moments the rigorous necessity of art. Thus his poetry deeply satisfies us even though its "subject matter" demoralizes us. In the same way that the opening notes of "Some of These Days" seem finally to say to Roquentin: "Il faut faire comme nous, souffrir *en mesure*," Reverdy's poems seem to invite us to give our despair their shape, their measure. Like the composer of the song and its singer, Reverdy and his reader "se sont lavés du péché d'exister." Both Roquentin and Reverdy know that a song (or any work of art) "n'existe pas, puisqu'elle n'a rien de trop: C'est tout le reste qui est trop par rapport à elle. Elle *est*." What the poet had intuited at the beginning of his career, Sartre's hero discovers at the end of his quest: everything that exists wears out, crumbles bit by bit toward nothingness, and only that which, like the melody, lies behind or beyond "L'existant qui tombe d'un présent à l'autre" remains "jeune et ferme." Long before Roquentin's "illumination" and subsequent understanding of his nausea, Reverdy had shown with his poetry that we no longer exist but are when we suffer the pain of our deepest malaise "en mesure, sans complaisance, sans pitié pour [nous]-même[s], avec une aride pureté."[35]

4. SYMBOLISM, CUBISM AND EXISTENTIALISM

At this point I should like to consider, briefly, a poem that neatly fuses the three aspects of Reverdy's poetry that we have been examining, the Symbolist, the Cubist and the Existentialist. "Départ," from *Les Ardoises du toit* (1918), typifies the short, overtly fragmentary manner of Reverdy's verse production during the 1915-1930 period:

> L'horizon s'incline
> > Les jours sont plus longs
> > Voyage
> Un coeur saute dans une cage
> > Un oiseau chante
> > Il va mourir
> Une autre porte va s'ouvrir
> > Au fond du couloir
> > Où s'allume
> > Une étoile
> Une femme brune
> > La lanterne du train qui part   (*PT*, p. 185)

The title, together with the bisyllabic, assonance-producing third line, "Voyage," roots "Départ" securely in nineteenth-century literature but especially in Baudelaire, who, it will be recalled, accords the theme of the voyage a privileged role in his poetry. Reverdy's text is also of course reminiscent of Rimbaud's *Illumination* of the same name, even if in the present instance the term is hardly bathed in "l'affection et le bruit neufs" as it is in Rimbaud's "Départ." More specifically Symbolist features of Reverdy's "Départ" include an overall elegiac tone, intimations of evening and perhaps death (not unlike "Le Soir"), the amalgam of vagueness and precise detail, an atmosphere of reverie and the generalized yearning for something beyond the here and now that almost inevitably accompanies the voyage motif.

The Cubist dimension of "Départ" inheres primarily in the

poem's visual-graphic form or, more accurately, in what this form implies. As with "Drame," one is immediately struck by the poem's apparent lack of any discursive or anecdotal thread. Seemingly disconnected and patently unequal verses merely follow one another without benefit of logical links or a stable leftside justification to unify them. By virtue of its isolated quality, each line-fragment is removed from and purified of any manifest context outside the poem. Hence, whatever latent meaning a given line-fragment may have will arise from its function within the structure of the poem. Parallels with Cubist esthetics, already noted in the case of "Drame," are obvious: the refusal of one-point perspective, the use of the conceptualization process and the ascendancy of structural over representational considerations.

It is through its structure and its texture that "Départ" reveals its kinship with Existentialist modes of thinking and feeling, particularly as these inform *La Nausée* and *Le Mythe de Sisyphe*. In spite of its disjointed appearance, "Départ" has both formal and substantive cohesiveness. Its prosodic structure, in fact, requires us to view its abbreviated verses in relation to one another; the twelve line-fragments thinly disguise a seven-line poem consisting of one alexandrine and six octosyllables, with the rhyme (or assonance) falling at the end of each new line thus created and the last line rhyming with the title. A single albeit floating persona, moreover, draws the fragments into a whole. Someone about to embark on a trip, records, in free-association fashion, the things, events, thoughts and feelings that he apprehends or experiences while seated in his compartment as his train leaves a station. But the departing traveler is not rounded-out; instead he remains shadowy and anonymous. We cannot even be certain that he is there; still, the gaze and the anxious thorax attest to the presence of some human, organizing force. Thus a kind of tension or precarious equipoise between concentration and dispersion, unity and fragmentation, defines "Départ."

The title of the poem provides the key to the specific nature

of the tension. The term "départ," when compared for ex-
ample with the phrase "l'invitation au voyage," seems coldly
neutral and precise; it offers no hint of Baudelaire's "luxe,
calme et volupté." In Reverdy's poem there is only the mo-
ment of actual departure or separation, of movement abruptly
imposed upon stillness. The line "Il va mourir," at the poem's
approximate center, speaks unequivocally of imminent, defini-
tive departure, of impending, final transition. The first line of
the poem, "L'horizon s'incline," contains the image of slip-
ping, nodding, falling that turns up again and again in Re-
verdy as the embodiment of dissolution and that anticipates, as
we have seen, the climactic pages of *La Nausée*. "Un coeur
saute dans une cage," the poem's most explicit metaphor, adds
an element of pathos through a highly compressed rendering of
pointless human struggle, prefiguring thereby Sartre's defini-
tion of man as a "passion inutile." The verse "La Lanterne du
train qui part" closes the poem with a half-echo of the title,
stressing gently but insistently the in-progress quality of the
somehow ominous and irreversible act of separation.

If somewhat muted by a Symbolist aura and Cubist tech-
niques, the poet's vision in "Départ" is essentially similar to
that found in "Ruine achevée." In both of these texts, as in his
entire *oeuvre*, Reverdy makes us see the entropic vision that he
shares with Sartre and Camus for what it is, the final validation
of multiple viewpoints and splintered personae in art and liter-
ature, Cubism's metaphysical base.

II. Francis Ponge

In a broad, primarily philosophical, sense, Francis Ponge represents paradoxically both a fulfillment and a refutation of Reverdy's promise. Especially when viewed in the perspective adopted in the preceding chapter, Reverdy's work tends to bear out the generally unexceptionable claim that "we in the United States are . . . unaccustomed to the appearance of a philosophical poet—a redundancy in France. . . . Philosophical pursuits . . . are not eccentric commitments: to the French poet they are the very matter that he exploits artistically."[1] If anything, Ponge's writings are even more suffused with philosophical overtones and associations than Reverdy's and thus even more typical of the philosophically-oriented poetry that seems so natural a feature of the literary landscape of France. Born in 1899, ten years after Reverdy, Ponge, like Reverdy, defined his position at one point in his career by alluding through parody to Descartes' famous *Cogito, ergo sum*:

> Puisque tu me lis, cher lecteur, donc je suïs; puisque tu nous lis (mon livre et moi), cher lecteur, donc nous sommes (Toi, lui et moi).[2]

Thus, while Reverdy transforms "Je pense, donc je suis" into "Je ne pense pas, je note," Ponge says, in effect, "J'écris, tu me lis, donc je suis." In the present chapter I shall first of all explore some of the implications inherent in these convergences and divergences involving Reverdy and Ponge. Then, within a chronological overview of the critical reaction to Ponge, I shall offer a brief critique of Sartre's seminal inquiry into Ponge's earlier writings. Finally (and principally), I shall attempt to elucidate the significance for his work as a whole of the reservations Ponge has expressed regarding *Le Mythe de Sisyphe*, the philosophical essay that also served as a major touchstone for my discussion of Reverdy.

I. REVERDY AND PONGE

Through a combination of intuition and deductive reasoning, Descartes, France's greatest philosopher, proves to himself that he exists by taking cognizance of the fact that he thinks, by reflecting upon his reflexive consciousness, whose existence he had derived from his methodic doubt. Thinking, moreover, is considered a faculty of the soul and as such completely separate from the body and from material reality generally. The idea of doubt leads Descartes to the notion of imperfection which, in turn, suggests both its opposite, perfection, and the source of perfection, God. Since a perfect Being could, logically, never deceive us, the evidence of our senses must be reliable and the external world consequently real. Reverdy, though committed to methodological thinking (witness the corpus of his theoretical writings), undermines the autonomous, spiritual status thought enjoys in Descartes by shifting our attention from the internal workings of the mind to the immediate transcription of perception:

> Quoi qu'il doive advenir de l'art et de la poésie, dont on prévoit couramment désormais la désuétude, il est certain qu'en ce domaine, on sera allé très loin dans l'aventure. . . . le poème est devenu la transcription des mots, des phrases, des images qui se présentent à la conscience du poète au moment où il écrit. . . . Ce qui a disparu c'est le discours, le thème, l'histoire à raconter. Il ne s'agit plus de rien raconter, mais de noter, de fixer, presque en guise de témoignage, ce qui a eu lieu, ce qui s'est déroulé dans la conscience.[3]

According to Reverdy, as we saw in the preceding chapter, the door to the poet's deepest self must somehow stand ajar to a world whose reality is never doubted. For Reverdy, writing, the creative act itself, consists of transcribing the fleeting activity of a consciousness that is imbedded in the world. Ponge, as we shall see, goes considerably further than Reverdy in exalting the act of writing over the operations of the mind, or, more precisely, in erasing the line that usually separates thought from action "in the world," as well as in fusing the experimental with the experiential.

If Descartes is the archetypal rationalist and Reverdy the virtuoso scribe or note-taker, Ponge is the *scripteur* (one of his own characterizations of himself)[4] *par excellence*. Occasionally in his theoretical pronouncements he echoes Reverdy. Both men, for example, draw a distinction between representational and non-representational writing simply by dropping the prefix of "représenter." But unlike Reverdy, Ponge invariably stresses the importance of words in their own right.[5] He believes, moreover, that "nous sommes à l'intérieur du monde humain, nous sommes à l'intérieur des paroles" (E, 190). Neither Reverdy nor Ponge can be accused of solipsism, and like Théophile Gautier, both are poets for whom the outer world exists.[6] But Ponge alone of the two maintains that "les mots sont aussi un monde extérieur" (E, 169).

There are other points of apparent contact but actual divergence between Reverdy and Ponge. To the degree that he produced his texts by juggling metrical and perhaps even lexical clichés, Reverdy grounds his poetic diction in literature, not life. At the same time, however, he obviously writes in the name of something beyond the text he produces, if only that of a failed quest for some transcendent meaning, or of the anguish that ensues from the admission of such a failure. Also, his poetic theory and the visual-graphic form of his verse notwithstanding, Reverdy's practice consistently leans toward the referential, as my reading of his work would, I trust, indicate. In the final analysis, the logic of reference, not that of allegory (in Paul de Man's sense of the latter term), governs Reverdy's poems. Perhaps this is so because while he identified with the pure poetry tradition, he never accepted the current within it which elevated the creative process and the act of composition above the created work, and which chose literature over life as the source of poetry. Contact with prior art teaches the poet his métier, according to Reverdy, but only contact with life itself allows the poet to function and produce in his métier:

> Il est vrai . . . que le poète naissant va d'abord vers l'oeuvre d'art—et c'est juste. . . . Mais . . . s'il n'a pas le pouvoir de garder le contact puissant avec la vie—s'il n'est pas en communion peut-être douloureuse mais profondément intime avec elle . . . il trébuchera au seuil de l'expression et sa plume ne tracera autre chose que des lignes de cendre sur une feuille de papier.[7]

By comparison, Ponge's "literariness" is much more thorough-going. For example, despite his celebrated *chosisme* (*Le Parti pris des choses*, published in 1942, being still the work that most people first associate with his name), Ponge's texts are fundamentally allegorical, free of dependent reference to an exterior (or, for that matter, inner) reality. Ponge "takes the side of things" in part simply to reveal the untransparent nature of even blatantly descriptive writing, the opacity of the most instrumental discourse.[8] Also, while in a general sense Reverdy's theory and practice illustrate the paired decline of the representational function and the ordering center of consciousness in poetry, an organizing presence has not disappeared altogether from his verse. Rather, it has been fractured to a point not quite beyond recognition. In Ponge's texts, on the other hand, the loss of the author's self as a center of consciousness is complete, and the only self that structures the text is the reader's. "C'est seulement . . . le lecteur qui fait le livre, lui-même, en le lisant" (*E*, 192), he asserts, and correctly so as far as his own practice is concerned. "La Mounine," from *La Rage de l'expression* (first published in 1952),[9] is a typical Ponge text in which the reader's role is a structuring, creative one. The act of reading, of submitting oneself fully to the processes and inner reverberations of *this* text is what changes it from the "Note après coup sur un ciel de Provence" (the sub-title of "La Mounine") into the "Poème après Coup sur un Ciel de Provence," which the "author" (i.e., the "je" and "nous" of the text) admits, significantly, in the final paragraph not to have finished.

Other inferences can be drawn from Ponge's belief that the reader "makes" the book. In an interview with Ponge, Philippe Sollers has made the following astute observation: "Il me semble très significatif que, quand vous décrivez la manière dont vous écrivez, vous traciez une configuration où l'auteur, le lecteur et le texte forment une sorte de triangle" (*E*, 87). If Reverdy is en route to monism, particularly in his theoretical pronouncements, the assumption that all existence divides into ego and world is still operative enough in him to shape his poetry in a fundamental way. In Ponge, on the other hand, Descartes' dualism, the subject-object dichotomy, has truly been transcended. A seamless web connects writer to text to reader, each of whom (or of which) comes into being, as in a triangle, by virtue of the other two's coming into being. And this triangle, the "toi, lui et moi" of Ponge's revision of Descartes' *Cogito*, this formulation in action, is an integral, functioning part of the only world man can know, the one he creates for himself. At this point one must wonder whether Robert Motherwell's neat summary of the Cubist revolution in painting is not more applicable to Ponge than to Reverdy:

Sometime in 1909 or 1910 Picasso took the great step . . . and pierced the "skin" of objects, reducing them and the world in which they existed to what we would now call subjective process. With this step Cubism snapped traditional Naturalism. Working with great intelligence, stubbornness and objectivity, they stumbled over the leading insight of the 20th century: all thought and feeling is relative to man, he does not reflect the world but invents it.[10]

Indeed, Ponge seems even readier than Reverdy to accept fully the esthetic stance implicit in Motherwell's reference to "subjective process" and man's "inventing" the world.

Such a convergence of views between Ponge and the Cubists should not surprise us. Like Reverdy (and many another twentieth-century French poet), Ponge has written extensively on the plastic arts, including essays on Picasso and Braque (no fewer than six on the latter).[11] And like Reverdy, his admiration for the twin giants of Cubism knows virtually no bounds. Where Reverdy asserts that "ce que Descartes avait fait dans le domaine philosophique Picasso . . . le renouvela dans le domaine de l'art,"[12] Ponge proclaims Picasso to be "comme un porte-drapeau de l'offensive intellectuelle" (*E*, 91).

Picasso for his part, according to Ponge, liked *Le Parti pris des choses* but preferred *La Rage de l'expression*, the work in which Ponge claims to place "sur la table de travail, la pratique scripturale, l'acte textuel" (*E*, 97). This emphasis on the productive process situates Ponge far closer to Valéry than to Reverdy. With regard to Ponge's stress on the production of the text, Sollers has observed: "Il n'y a plus valorisation de l'objet fini, mais accentuation mise sur la production elle-même. . . ." (*E*, 96). Sollers has also spoken of the "primat du signifiant" in Ponge (*E*, 60). It seems not unfaithful to Sollers's thinking here to merge these observations and affirm the primacy of the *production* of the signifier in Ponge. The signified interests him not at all, and the signifier increasingly interests him only as it calls attention to itself aborning. For a text's only "message" is encoded not in the inscription but in the production of the inscription, and it is by retracing the productive process that reader replaces author, thereby closing the author-text-reader triangle.

In spite of his admiration for Picasso and the Cubists, however, Ponge situates the last great esthetico-ideological revolution in France around 1870 (*E*, 94), not 1910 as Motherwell and Reverdy would tend to do. Accomplishing the revolution of 1870 Ponge sees Lautréamont and Rimbaud in poetry (with Baudelaire earlier and Mallarmé later) and Cézanne in painting (with Manet earlier and the Cubists later). He admires Lautréamont because the latter rejects personal poetry, urges that criticism address itself to the shape (*forme*) and not the substance (*fond*) of a writer's ideas and sentences, and because he treats these and related matters in a work entitled *Poésies*.[13] In Ponge's view, when the title of Lautréamont's work, *Poésies*, is examined in relation to its contents, the work as a whole suggests that poetry itself is the only fit subject for poetry and that genre distinctions are irrelevant, notions which Ponge finds particularly congenial.

Not surprisingly, these very beliefs are also held by another admirer of Lautréamont, Philippe Sollers,[14] who was perhaps the single most important figure involved in Ponge's rediscovery in the early 1960's. Convinced as I am that inspecting Ponge's literary fortunes, including the circumstances of his rediscovery in the early 1960's, is an especially reliable way of approaching his uniqueness as a writer, I shall now review his *oeuvre* in terms of the changing critical reaction it inspired from the 1920's to the 1960's.

2. THE CRITICAL REACTION

Francis Ponge has been "discovered" as a writer on three different occasions at intervals of about twenty years, originally by the *Nouvelle Revue Française* circle (Jean Paulhan, Jacques Rivière, etc.) during the 1920's, then by Sartre in 1944, and finally by the magazine *Tel Quel* in the early sixties. His third "discovery" has proved more durable than the earlier two, in part no doubt because it coincided with Gallimard's launching the publication of what will presumably be Ponge's complete works.[15] Also, while he is obviously grateful even now for the attention he received early on from the *Nouvelle Revue Française* and later from Sartre, Ponge has found the *Tel Quel* approach to

his work the most compatible of the three with his own con-
victions as a writer. Yet—and Ponge himself would no doubt
be the first to acknowledge this—general interest in and a
deepening understanding of his work dates from the two-part
essay entitled "A propos du *Parti pris des choses*" that Sartre
published on him (in *Poésie*, numbers 20 and 21) in 1944.
Moreover, except possibly for Marcel Spada's superb mono-
graph,[16] Sartre's essay, retitled "L'Homme et les choses" for
inclusion in volume one of *Situations*,[17] is probably still the
most brilliant and suggestive study to have been written thus
far on Ponge. For this reason, and also because of a blind spot
at its center that can perhaps be turned into an insight, I shall
examine this study rather carefully. Before doing that, how-
ever, I should like to consider briefly Ponge's earliest "dis-
covery," that of the *NRF* group in the 1920's.

In 1970 the Gallimard and Seuil publishing houses jointly
issued *Entretiens de Francis Ponge avec Philippe Sollers*, a book
which comprises the transcripts of twelve lengthy radio inter-
views that Sollers conducted with Ponge during the spring of
1967. As we have already seen, these interviews are an invalu-
able source of information about Ponge, especially as regards
his conception of what he has been trying to do in his writing
for the last half century. In one of the interviews he goes into
some detail concerning his relations with the *NRF* during the
early 1920's. He tells how the magazine, after commenting fa-
vorably in its pages on some texts that he had published in
another review, then accepted for its own pages "Trois sa-
tires," three texts which were, in Ponge's words, "très axés
vers l'action, une action satirique, la littérature étant par moi
considérée comme une arme, à ce moment-là" (p. 62). Later in
the same interview Ponge talks about his second attempt, this
time unsuccessful, to publish texts in the *NRF*:

> Il est très significatif que le second groupe de textes que j'ai
> envoyé à *La Nouvelle Revue Française* après l'acceptation des

premiers, eh bien c'était un groupe de textes, très brefs et qui auraient pu être imprimés en italique, comme des poèmes, mais qui étaient axés sur les problèmes du langage à proprement parler. Il y en avait un qui s'appelait: "Du logoscope," c'est-à-dire "regardez le logos," "regardez les mots" et dont le sujet, comme on dit, était *un mot*, comme le mot "souvenir," où il y a des consonnes, *s*, *v*, *n*, *r*, qui me semblaient être quelque chose comme son squelette, et puis des voyelles, *o*, *u*, *e*, *i*, qui me semblaient comme sa chair. (pp. 65-66)

Ces textes ont eu beaucoup de difficulté à être admis. Jacques Rivière, qui n'était pas encore mort, mais il était déjà gravement malade et il devait mourir de cette maladie, avait accepté "Du logoscope," mais une difficulté s'était élevée entre nous au sujet de l'importance des caractères, parce que je désirais que chacun de mes textes, puisqu'ils étaient rares, fasse effet et donc soit publié dans des caractères vaniteux. Eh bien, il s'est élevé une difficulté.

Paulhan, qui est venu à la suite de Rivière, n'a pas publié ces textes, qui sont restés enfouis pendant des années, que je n'ai retrouvés que plus tard. (p. 67)

What is significant in all this, and not a little ironic, is that Ponge's satirical pieces were accepted by the *NRF*, while his earliest metapoetic efforts were, for whatever reason, ultimately rejected. Why ironic? Because in retrospect, that is, from the vantage point of today, it is clear that the authentic or characteristic Ponge is the Ponge of "Du logoscope," not the Ponge of "Trois satires." Gallimard, publisher of *La Nouvelle Revue Française*, did bring out Ponge's slim plaquette entitled *Douze petits écrits* in 1926, but with that single exception the poet would have to wait nearly two decades for another serious launching on the sea of French letters.

Ponge's second "discovery," by Sartre in 1944, would prove to be vastly more important for him than his abortive dis-

covery at the hands of the *NRF* had been some twenty years
before. Sartre's essay abounds in illuminating observations. He
points out, for example, that "Ponge se doit de décrire en
courant, à l'intérieur même de sa phrase, les éléments qui
composent la 'chose' étudiée et leur genèse. Ainsi y a-t-il des
choses dans la chose et des genèses de la genèse" (pp. 276-77).
Stressing as it does the importance of the notion of genesis for
Ponge, this statement gets closer perhaps to the heart of Ponge
than does anything else Sartre has to say. The very pertinence
of this quotation, however, is misleading since generally Sartre
seems not to have grasped the true nature and import of
Ponge's *oeuvre*, and in fact elsewhere in his study Sartre con-
tradicts what he says here.

The original title of his essay, "A propos du *Parti pris des
choses*," points to one of the probable reasons behind Sartre's
eventually unreliable reading of Ponge. Almost everything
Sartre says about his subject is keyed into *Le Parti pris des choses*
(1942), a book which in at least two important respects is
atypical of its author. First of all, rare is the work by Ponge
whose title is not literal and in that sense self-referring (e.g.,
Douze petits écrits, *Proêmes*, *Le Grand Recueil*, *Tome premier*,
Nouveau recueil). And one would search in vain to find another
Ponge title so insistently *chosiste*. Secondly, and with respect
now to the book's contents, the texts that go to make up *Le
Parti pris des choses*, particularly the shorter ones, are (except
possibly for some in *Pièces*, the third volume of *Le Grand Re-
cueil*) considerably more polished, more finished, than are the
bulk of Ponge's texts. In general, Ponge's writings are longer,
both more open and more intricate in construction and more
turned in on themselves than are nearly all the pieces in *Le
Parti pris des choses*.[18] In Sartre's defense it should be pointed
out that none of this was as obvious or even as true in 1944 as
it is today; at the present time we have ready access to perhaps
ten times as much Ponge material as Sartre could possibly have
seen in 1944.

Sartre's misreading of Ponge also has to do with the two men's respective attitudes toward language and writing. In *L'Etre et le néant*, which Sartre published in 1943, the year before his essay on Ponge appeared, he speaks of language as a tool, a "technique," as he puts it, which is dead once it is not being spoken.[19] For Ponge, on the other hand, French is a living, growing organism which he calls "la Françité,"[20] a tree whose trunk is Malherbe and whose topmost leaf at the moment is himself. He says, for example, in *Pour un Malherbe*: "ce livre est une production de la langue française, qui croît, pour ainsi dire, à travers lui" (p. 257). Furthermore, though autonomous, Ponge's texts are not hard, burnished verbal icons. Rather, they are, in Ponge's own terminology, "objeux" (a neologism that contracts "objet" and "jeu de mots"), endlessly amusing (i.e., witty and engrossing) and highly self-conscious verbal acts. They are more "poèmes-laboratoires" than "poèmes-objets." It is this crucial aspect of Ponge's texts that Sartre fails to appreciate sufficiently, and when he does speak of it, he says, somewhat disapprovingly, "ces phrases si drues . . . sont allégées et comme évidées par une sorte de gaminerie bonhomme qui se glisse partout" (*Situations*, I, p. 278). Because Sartre virtually dismisses out of hand Ponge's "légèreté heureuse à l'égard du langage" (*Situations*, I, p. 277), he attributes to the texts of *Le Parti pris des choses* a quality or a tendency they do not in fact possess.

More than once Sartre expresses his belief that in *Le Parti pris des choses* "le solide prédomine," that if Ponge loves living creatures, "c'est à condition de les pétrifier." He then suggests a possible explanation for this tendency on Ponge's part: "Peut-être derrière son entreprise révolutionnaire est-il permis d'entrevoir un grand rêve nécrologique: celui d'ensevelir tout ce qui vit, l'homme surtout, dans le suaire de la matière." What is so astonishing about Sartre's "nécrologique" reading of Ponge is that it runs exactly counter to what is perhaps the central image in Ponge's *oeuvre*, that of birth. Further on in

Sartre's essay we discover the mind-set that predisposed him to
arrive at this reading. Using the language of *L'Etre et le néant*,
he asserts that Ponge seems simply to have chosen "un moyen
rapide de réaliser symboliquement notre désir commun d'exis-
ter enfin sur le type de l'en-soi. Ce qui le fascine dans la chose,
c'est son mode d'existence, sa totale adhésion à soi, son repos"
(*Situations*, I, pp. 286-88). If there is one characteristic
Ponge's texts do not have it is that of repose.

Sartre's difficulty with Ponge, his blind spot, derives from
his philosophical orientation and from his assuming the texts
of *Le Parti pris des choses* to be primarily referential when they
are not, when Ponge's *chosisme* is purely methodological. Ac-
cording to Sartre, Ponge unwittingly applies in his work
"l'axiome qui est à l'origine de toute la Phénoménologie: 'Aux
choses mêmes' " (*Situations*, I, pp. 262-63), and he concludes
his essay by claiming that "Ponge poète . . . a jeté les bases
d'une Phénoménologie de la Nature" (*Situations*, I, p. 293).
Ponge's writing does resemble that of a phenomenologist. He
worries over things rather than feelings. He prefers halting de-
scription to sure interpretation or explanation. Instead of in-
gesting the world with Romantic omnivorousness, his con-
sciousness seems to "explode toward" the world in phe-
nomenological fashion. However, what ultimately interests
Ponge is not the given, the primary concern of the phenome-
nologist, but the given's potential as a source of language in
action. Sartre fails to see that Ponge has taken the side of
things as a way of shortcircuiting any desire he might feel
while writing to express an idea or an emotion. As Ponge him-
self pointed out in an interview published (in English) in
1969: "I have chosen things, objects, so that I would always
have a brake on my subjectivity."[21]

Ultimately of course it is not things that interest Ponge but
words, as the *Tel Quel* group helped show when they, in their
turn, "discovered" Ponge in the 1960's. The *Tel Quel* writers
shared their discovery by publishing texts by and about Ponge

in their magazine, and by writing the first two book-length studies of his work in French.[22] It should also be noted that *Entretiens de Francis Ponge avec Philippe Sollers*, which appeared in 1970, resulted directly from Ponge's contact with the *Tel Quel* group. Today, this series of interviews seems the most important contribution the *Tel Quel* group made to the cause of Francis Ponge. For Ponge, one of the most methodical of poetic adventurers, is his own best critic and nowhere is he in better critical form than in these interviews. In his third *entretien* with Sollers, for example, he sets forth what has always been his purpose: "je n'ai jamais cherché qu'à redonner à la langue française cette densité, cette matérialité, cette épaisseur (mystérieuse, bien sûr) qui lui vient de ses origines les plus anciennes. . . . et entrer profondément dans ce monde aussi concret . . . aussi sensible pour moi que pouvaient l'être les paysages, les architectures, les événements, les personnes, les *choses* du monde dit physique" (p. 47). The key phrase in this passage is "mystérieuse, bien sûr," for Ponge aspires to explore the essential mystery of the mother tongue.

Language as an historical and living phenomenon, as both inscription and speech, is the starting and end point of Ponge's writing. Littré's *Dictionary*, not life, is his primary source, a kind of total dictionary (illustrated, etymological, analogical, etc.), his goal.[23] His texts, as he tells us in "Le Soleil placé en abîme" (in *Le Grand Recueil: Pièces*, pp. 151-88), will be "objeux," infinitely intricate and endlessly spinning wheels within wheels, text-cogs whose gears mesh in the great "horlogerie universelle." This vast universal clockworks, he also informs us, is our only real homeland, and it is charted and made habitable by formulation.

Formulation in what sense? As self-conscious becoming, as self-regarding and inceptive verbal act, as utterance resounding right now out of silence, writing tracing right here across the page—hence formulation less as the fact of words than as their knowing birth. For Ponge, language is opaque and inexhaustible, and yet at the same time penetrable and inviting. Our mother tongue, furthermore, is our fatherland. It is where we belong since it is where we come from and what will live on, enriched perhaps by us, after we are gone. It is our contact with the absolute, since it is everywhere at hand yet always disclosing new aspects of itself to us. To attend to it is to witness countless unveilings, births, words emerging from other words, especially at the literal and the root levels.

Significantly, the longer Ponge lives the more he seems bent on publishing his workbooks, throwing open the doors to his *atelier* and displaying his sketches to the public, so that we all might somehow be present, as it were, at the birth of texts already "born." In 1971 he published *La Fabrique du pré* (Genève: Skira), the workbook for "Le Pré," a text that was first published in 1964 (in *Tel Quel*). *La Fabrique du pré* is thus in a sense the afterbirth of "Le Pré." It is the matrix-factory exposed to our leisurely and pleasurable gaze, it is the time-machine that allows us to go back to the rise into form (the formulation), the genesis (to echo Sartre) of the text which Beth Archer Brombert has characterized as Ponge's "magnum opus to date."[24] "Le Pré," a long, lushly elaborated *objeu* which will be discussed in detail in part three of this chapter, very soon focuses not on the meadow but on all the possible textual permutations and combinations that the word-particle *pré* inspires in Ponge, and, not unlike its workbook, gravitates ever back to earlier, preparatory moments, greenness, awakening cries, swellings and original explosions.

Two illuminating paradoxes now become apparent. As we come forward in time following Ponge's steadily improving literary fortunes, we realize that Ponge himself, by both the rhythm of his publications and the specific textuality of each of his *objeux*, seems to invite us to go backwards in time in order to see the birth of ever earlier texts and previous verbal moments. "Joca Seria," for example, published in 1967 (in *Nouveau recueil*, pp. 53-96), comprises the extensive notes

Ponge took in preparation for writing a rather short piece on Giacometti, an essay that was published long before the appearance of "Joca Seria." *Pour un Malherbe*, which appeared in 1965, is to a large extent the journal or journals for a book on Malherbe that Ponge was writing in the 1950's but which never saw print. *Proêmes*, brought out in 1948, is a combination gloss-commentary-notebook for *Le Parti pris des choses*, which dates from 1942. Thus the relationship between "Le Pré" and *La Fabrique du pré*, including their order of publication, is more or less typical of Ponge. With each of the foregoing pairs, the later publication was actually written before the earlier publication. In all cases the "finished" text and its workbook, whether taken together or separately, send us back to beginnings, to earlier versions, to first formulations.

The other of the two paradoxes I referred to above is perhaps implicit in the one I have just discussed. As we come forward in time with Ponge, as we move with him through his texts from his twenties to his seventies, we discover that it is not decline and death, not Thanatos, that we are approaching, but rather endless renewal, Eros itself.

3. METAPOET

An obsessive concern with its own constituent elements, its words, dominates Francis Ponge's poetry. This trait, which should not be confused with narcissism, appears in many guises and contexts, and yet it always manages to illuminate some aspect of a single, coherent vision. Scrutinizing Ponge's self-consciousness, we make out the contours of his vision. As we do, we realize that his work has a special relevance for our time. We also realize that Ponge's self-regarding stance as a poet shapes the way in which Eros governs his writing, and at the same time sets him beyond the reach of the Existentialist "souci" or "peur" that haunted Reverdy.

In part because of their pervasive self-consciousness, Ponge's texts hardly conform to most conceptions of what poems, even prose poems, are or should be. They contain puns, false starts, repetitions, agendas, recapitulations, syllogistic overtones, a heavy ideological content, and other features that one normally associates with prose—and the prose of argumentation at that—rather than with poetry. Nevertheless, Ponge is without question a poet, but one who has moved so far away from both the pure poetry and the "art for art's sake" traditions, as well as from the Symbolist heritage generally, that we must alter our notions of what poetry is, or can be, in order to consider him a poet.

Except for individual pieces scattered throughout his work, *Proêmes* (1948) is the most "unpoetic" and explicitly ideological of Ponge's "poetic" efforts.[25] We find in this collection numerous texts that tell us what it is he is arguing for. We discover, for example, that the two basic premises from which Ponge starts to write are givens which would prevent virtually any other would-be writer from even picking up his pen. These premises, patently of the extreme absurdist type, are that the world is utterly meaningless and that language is an inherently unreliable means of expression (*TP*, p. 221). In this connection it should be noted that an important sequence in *Proêmes*, grouped under the title "Pages bis," constitutes an avowed rebuttal or completion of *Le Mythe de Sisyphe*. While Ponge accepts most of what Camus says as valid, he criticizes the latter for not including among his "thèmes de l'absurde" the unreliability of language and for not freeing himself of his "nostalgie de l'*un*," of his longing for a single, underlying principle that would justify everything (*TP*, pp. 203-34, *passim*).

"Fable," which belongs to a group of texts in *Proêmes* written considerably earlier than "Pages bis,"[26] is one of the poet's most revealing as far as his views on the limits of language are concerned:

Par le mot *par* commence donc ce texte
Dont la première ligne dit la vérité,
Mais ce tain sous l'une et l'autre
Peut-il être toléré?
Cher lecteur déjà tu juges
Là de nos difficultés . . .

(APRES *sept ans de malheurs*
Elle brisa son miroir.) (TP, p. 144)

The title alone suggests that here is a "story" that contains a "lesson." As we shall see, the "story" in "Fable" is that of Ponge's traumatic disillusionment with language as a reliable means of expression, while its "lesson" or "moral" is his implied solution to the problem of language's unreliability, a solution that is actualized or realized by the text itself.

The entire poem is governed by a principle of reversal. As we read "Fable," instead of being led on from one line to the next, we are continuously thrown back toward the beginning. The sense of the first line, for example, is such that we gravitate to its first word rather than its last. The second line sends us back to the first, lines three and four refer back to lines one and two together, and the next two lines invite us to reflect on the questions raised thus far, with "déjà" and "Là" in lines five and six, after "donc," "Dont," "Mais" and "il" (among other words) in lines one through four, serving as the calls to a retrospective reading of the text. In the poem's last two lines, the first word, entirely capitalized, is the one to which we are inevitably drawn back. In addition, the normal order of events is reversed here, for an effect (seven years of bad luck) precedes its cause (the act of breaking a mirror). The last two lines, moreover, stand apart from the rest of the poem and are in parentheses because they represent a complete change of tone—the literal and the serene have given way to the fabulous and the violent—and they are emphasized because they make ex-

plicit what is implicit in lines one through six, which they ob-
lige us to reread.

The reversal or movement backward that is operative
throughout "Fable" is a metaphor for the return to the con-
crete which Ponge would like language to accomplish, and it
is at odds with the traditional metaphor, also present in "Fa-
ble," that assimilates language to a mirror on the grounds that
both are simply faithful reflectors of reality and endowed with
no opacity of their own. To see this conflict, and its resolution,
we must go through the poem again. The first two lines, play-
fully self-conscious, are in a most literal sense true, and they
are literal to the point of referring to nothing beyond them-
selves. In their perfect unpretentiousness they show us that
words which have been stripped of their figurative dimension
and of their referential function can still have meaning. But
lines three and four tend to reduce even further, if not to elim-
inate altogether, the radically diminished scope of the first two
lines, for they ask whether the assumption that underpins the
very existence of these lines can be tolerated. This assumption,
that language, like a mirror, is a neutral and therefore com-
pletely reliable medium, is dramatically rejected in the poem's
closing couplet. Meanwhile, in lines five and six, the reader
has been directly implicated in the dilemma, and properly so,
given the poem's "subject." Thus, on one level there is pro-
gression in "Fable," movement forward through a series of dis-
coveries that culminate in the exasperated gesture of someone's
shattering a mirror. But on another level, as we have seen,
there is retrogression, movement backward to the very first
word.

If the one process in "Fable," progression, leads to disillu-
sionment and failure, its obverse, retrogression, hints broadly
at a way out of the dilemma, at a solution to the problem of
language's unreliability. In this deceptively slight poem,
Ponge superimposes the one process on the other, and in so
doing implies that the two are inextricably related. By turning

away from the assumption that language is merely an instrument, he seems to say, we turn toward words in their own right, thereby restoring to them some of their original concreteness and immediacy. If in "Fable" Ponge declares the mirror-language metaphor to be invalid, he at the same time and in the same space enunciates a corollary to this declaration, that the symbolizing tendency of language, its apparently inexorable drift from the status of onomatopoeia to that of abstract sign, can and should be reversed. The poem's forward motion ends in destruction, the smashing of an idol, while its simultaneous backward movement stops ironically and yet fittingly at "Par," the most basic term of means or agency, which we now gaze upon in all its mysterious opacity. The way to deal with language's unreliability, its refusal to remain purely instrumental, Ponge would suggest, is to accept words for what they are, not as transparent means but as opaque ends, and to build from there. Before our very eyes he has converted an impasse, the one he would later chide Camus for not confronting, into a breakthrough, at least potentially.

As I have already noted, Ponge also criticizes Camus for his "nostalgie de l'*un*" (*TP*, p. 209). This criticism relates to Ponge's other starting premise, the meaninglessness of the world. His attitude vis-à-vis the world is profoundly anti-Platonic; nothing stands for or is a sign of anything beyond itself. The truth lies not in some ultimate Unity which we must strive to grasp, but in the endless and real variety of things which we must simply accept. We must outgrow our "nostalgie d'absolu" (*TP*, p. 244), absolutes being by definition unattainable anyway, as well as our need to interpret, to explicate or to decipher the world. A writer can and should simply describe the world in action by means of a "littérature littérante" (*TP*, p. 227).

Ponge well knows, of course, that things are ultimately opaque, forever immune to exhaustive description, and would remain so even if language did not invariably distort that which it claims to express. Clearly, then, he has a special kind of description in mind when he urges that description be practiced. What he envisages is a text in which "les ressources infinies de l'épaisseur des choses" are rendered by "les ressources infinies de l'épaisseur sémantique des mots" (*TP*, p. 200). He seeks a balance of equivalences, an equation between the order of things and the order of words. To achieve such a balance the poet must create a closed system of words that will recreate the specificity of the thing, its "qualité différentielle,"[27] in a dizzying complex of verbal games. In an important sense, therefore, Ponge's text will not be about the thing but about itself, about its own terms; it will be a "création métalogique" (*TP*, p. 220), a piece of writing whose internal relations are all, an end in itself.

Ponge has been writing "créations métalogiques" and, characteristically, studying his method of composition for more than a half-century. He published a number of his earliest efforts in this genre, all composed during the 1924-1939 period, in *Le Parti pris des choses* (1942). Over the years since the 1920's he has continued to refine his technique, to the point where some of his pieces of the 1950's and 1960's, such as "La Chèvre" and "Le Pré," are truly dazzling in their complexity. Soon after it first appeared in print, "La Chèvre" was brilliantly analyzed by B. M. Douthat.[28] "Le Pré," which was composed between 1960 and 1964,[29] may well be Ponge's most subtle "création métalogique" to date. Also, more explicitly than any other of his texts, it develops the implications and possibilities inherent in "Fable."

We shall examine "Le Pré" in some detail, but before we do we must turn our attention to another major text, "Le Soleil placé en abîme," which contains, among other things, passages in which Ponge sets forth his technique or method for writing "créations métalogiques." He christens the new genre with the apparently frivolous but in fact quite serious name of "l'Objeu," which contracts and synthesizes "objet" and "jeu de mots":

> . . . nous l'avons baptisé l'*Objeu*. C'est celui où l'objet de notre émotion placé d'abord en abîme, l'épaisseur vertigineuse et l'absurdité du langage, considérées seules, sont manipulées de telle façon que, par la multiplication intérieure des rapports, les liaisons formées au niveau des racines et les significations bouclées à double tour, soit créé ce fonctionnement qui seul peut rendre compte de la profondeur substantielle, de la variété et de la rigoureuse harmonie du monde. (*GRP*, p. 156)

Thus, Ponge aspires to create a verbal machine that will have as much local intricacy as its counterpart in the world of objects. The intricacy of such texts will derive from the multiple reciprocal relations of the words, particularly from their mutual reverberations at the root level. This new genre will give utterance to the depth, the variety, and the harmony of the world, by remaking, verbally and one by one, its component parts. As Ponge implies here and elsewhere, a thing and its formulation can be one, an identification or fusion which he feels poets alone make possible inasmuch as they alone "s'enfoncent dans la nuit du logos,—jusqu'à ce qu'enfin ils se retrouvent au niveau des RACINES, où se confondent les choses et les formulations."[30]

Ponge is especially intrigued by the sun because he sees it as "la grande roue" in our corner of "l'horlogerie universelle" (*GRP*, pp. 172, 176). The sun gave birth to our solar system, sustains all life in it and has destined everything in it to cool or run down and die one day. But the rhythmical manner in which the sun "temporarily" supports life, though tantalizing in the extreme, carries with it a crucial lesson. Each night prepares a new day, in every winter solstice is born the next summer's solstice. The whole rise-and-fall process in the lives of plants and animals, which the sun causes—since it "les fait gonfler, bander, éclater; jouir, germer; faner, défaillir et mourir" (*GRP*, p. 167)—is endlessly repeated. What we must do then is clear: we must "recommencer volontairement l'hymne" (*GRP*, p. 165); we must arbitrarily restart the cycle by choosing to sing the birth, the ascent out of darkness, the tumescence of everything. While we cannot forestall entropy, the eventual decline of everything into chaos, by concentrating on genesis, on life's thrust toward definition and differentiation, we gain a degree of control over our destiny. By focusing on and rejoicing in explosion and expression (in the etymological sense), we keep the final collapse of all and everything, including our own death, where it in fact is, outside or beyond our experience, where consciousness of the self in action cannot be.

Not surprisingly, the theme of birth haunts Ponge's writings. In *Pour un Malherbe* he goes so far as to define poetry as "le langage remis à son état naissant" (p. 275). In an essay on Braque's sketches he places himself among those who prefer "presque aux chefs-d'oeuvre ces feuillets d'albums, ces pages d'étude où s'inscrivent toutes vives les péripéties du combat avec l'ange, enfin ces communiqués quotidiens de la guerre sainte. . . ."[31] He is fascinated by Braque's sketches because they reflect stages in the development of the finished work, because they constitute a kind of record of the artist's labor pains. For the same reason he starts his long essay on Fautrier's "Les Otages" with a meditation on Michelangelo's "Slaves," four "unfinished" pieces of sculpture which, it will be recalled, depict four slaves straining mightily against both their chains and the granite block out of which they are emergent, half-hewn. Their dual goal, freedom and existence, is really one, for as they struggle to break out of their chains, they are also struggling to free themselves of a far graver servitude, that of non-differentiation. From nothingness, out of a uniform slab of stone, each slave pushes valiantly toward definition, toward the affirmation of self through form.

Ponge's closing observation on the "Slaves" is singularly revealing:

. . . ces esclaves ne seront jamais libres: leurs corps vieilliront dans leurs chaînes, ils s'y abîmeront, puis s'y décomposeront. Mais rien dans l'apparence fixée n'autorise cette idée, ce pronostic et le désespoir qui, pour le contemplateur, en résulte. (*TP*, p. 430)

At some hypothetical future time the slaves will doubtless die, still not free. But in their present posture, in their "apparence fixée," we see only their thrust upward into life. The artist's focus is on birth and creation, on shape declaring itself against the obliterating void. These are not works *in* progress, they are works *about* progress, about the transformation of nothing, stone, into something, sculpture. They are sculpture about sculpture, metasculpture, and this is why Ponge lingers on them.

This very theme, the birth of form, also turns up in many of Ponge's "créations métalogiques." We shall see it shortly, for example, in "Le Pré." In view of the prevalence of this theme throughout Ponge's work and in view of the theoretical statements that one finds in his practice (e.g., his definition of "l'objeu" in "Le Soleil placé en abîme"), we must ask ourselves whether the term "objeu" adequately conveys what Ponge in fact does in his imaginative (as opposed to his methodological or occasional) pieces. For these texts, besides attempting to formulate a thing's "qualité différentielle" through intricate word play, contain the principles of Ponge's *art poétique*. Furthermore, as just noted, they are concerned with the birth of form, with the creative moment. Ponge's "objeux" are thus at one and the same time "about" their own verbal selves, "about" the explosive rise of form, and "about" the principles of a poetic art. Since the term "metapoem" can suggest all three of these "subjects" and since the poet himself uses the phrase "création métalogique" in reference to his work, "métapoem" seems a more fitting label than "objeu" for the kind of text Ponge actually writes.

"Le Pré" is both a metapoem in the above senses of the term and a major recapitulation for Ponge. It is a relatively long text but such an important one that I quote it here in its entirety, numbering its stanzas so as to facilitate discussion:

(1) Que parfois la Nature, à notre réveil, nous propose
     Ce à quoi justement nous étions disposés,
     La louange aussitôt s'enfle dans notre gorge.
     Nous croyons être au paradis.

(2) Voilà comme il en fut du pré que je veux dire,
     Qui fera mon propos d'aujourd'hui.

(3) Parce qu'il s'y agit plus d'une façon d'être
     Que d'un plat à nos yeux servi,
     La parole y convient plutôt que la peinture
     Qui n'y suffirait nullement.

(4) Prendre un tube de vert, l'étaler sur la page,
     Ce n'est pas faire un pré.
     Ils naissent autrement.
     Ils sourdent de la page.
     Et encore faut-il que ce soit page brune.

(5) Préparons donc la page où puisse aujourd'hui naître
     Une vérité qui soit verte.

(6) Parfois donc—ou mettons aussi bien par endroits—
     Parfois, notre nature—
     J'entends dire, d'un mot, la Nature sur notre planète
     Et ce que, chaque jour, à notre réveil, nous sommes—
     Parfois, notre nature nous a préparé(s) (à) un pré.

(7)   Mais qu'est-ce, qui obstrue ainsi notre chemin?
       Dans ce petit sous-bois mi-ombre mi-soleil,
       Qui nous met ces bâtons dans les roues?
       Pourquoi, dès notre issue en surplomb sur la page,
       Dans ce seul paragraphe, tous ces scrupules?

(8)   Pourquoi donc, vu d'ici, ce fragment limité d'espace,
       Tiré à quatre rochers ou à quatre haies d'aubépines,
       Guère plus grand qu'un mouchoir,
       Moraine des forêts, ondée de signe adverse,
       Ce pré, surface amène, auréole des sources
       Et de l'orage initial suite douce
       En appel ou réponse unanime anonyme à la pluie,
       Nous semble-t-il plus précieux soudain
       Que le plus mince des tapis persans?

(9)   Fragile, mais non frangible,
       La terre végétale y reprend parfois le dessus,
       Où les petits sabots du poulain qui y galopa le
          marquèrent,
       Ou le piétinement vers l'abreuvoir des bestiaux qui
          lentement
       S'y précipitèrent . . .

(10) Tandis qu'une longue théorie de promeneurs
          endimanchés, sans y
       Salir du tout leurs souliers blancs, y procèdent
       Au long du petit torrent, grossi, de noyade, ou de
          perdition,
       Pourquoi donc, dès l'abord, nous tient-il interdits?

(11) Serions-nous donc déjà parvenus au naos,
       Enfin au lieu sacré d'un petit déjeuné de raisons?
       Nous voici, en tout cas, au coeur des pléonasmes
       Et au seul niveau logique qui nous convient.

(12) Ici tourne déjà le moulin à prières,
Sans la moindre idée de prosternation, d'ailleurs,
Car elle serait contraire aux verticalités de l'endroit.

(13) Crase de paratus, selon les étymologistes latins,
Près de la roche et du ru,
Prêt à faucher ou à paître,
Préparé pour nous par la nature,
Pré, paré, pré, près, prêt,

(14) Le pré gisant ici comme le participe passé par
   excellence
S'y révère aussi bien comme notre préfixe des préfixes,
Préfixes déjà dans préfixe, présent déjà dans présent.

(15) Pas moyen de sortir de nos onomatopées originelles.
Il faut donc y rentrer.

(16) Nul besoin, d'ailleurs, d'en sortir,
Leurs variations suffisant bien à rendre compte
De la merveilleusement fastidieuse
Monotonie et variété du monde,
Enfin, de sa perpétuité.

(17) Encore faut-il les prononcer.
Parler. Et, peut-être, paraboler.
Toutes, les dire.

    .   .   .   .

(18)   (Ici doit intervenir un long passage, où, dans la
manière un peu de l'interminable séquence de clavecin
solo du cinquième concerto brandebourgeois, c'est-à-
dire de façon fastidieuse et mécanique mais méca-
nisante à la fois, non tellement de la musique que
de la logique, raisonneuse, du bout des lèvres, non de
la poitrine ou du coeur, je tâcherai d'expliquer, je dis
bien expliquer, deux ou trois choses, et d'abord que si

le pré, dans notre langue, représente une des plus importantes et primordiales notions logiques qui soient, il en est de même sur le plan physique (géophysique), car il s'agit en vérité d'une métamorphose de l'eau, laquelle, au lieu de s'évaporer directement, à l'appel du feu, en nuages, choisit ici, se liant à la terre et en passant par elle, c'est-à-dire par les restes pétries du passé des trois règnes et en particulier par les granulations les plus fines du minéral, réimprégnant en somme le cendrier universel, de donner renaissance à la vie sous sa forme la plus élémentaire, l'herbe: élémentarité-alimentarité. Ce chapitre, qui sera *aussi* celui de la musique des prés, sonnera de façon grêle et minutieuse, avec une quantité d'appoggiatures, pour s'achever (s'il s'achève) en accelerando et rinforzando à la fois, jusqu'à une sorte de roulement de tonnerre où nous nous réfugierons dans les bois. Mais la perfection de ce passage pourrait me demander quelques années encore. Quoi qu'il en soit . . .)

.   .   .   .

(19)   L'orage originel a longuement parlé.

.   .   .   .

(20) L'orage originel n'aura-t-il donc en nous si longuement
        grondé
    Seulement pour qu'enfin
            —car il s'éloigne, n'occupant plus que
            partiellement l'horizon bas où il fulgure encore—
    Parant au plus urgent, allant au plus pressé,
    Nous sortions de ces bois,
    Passions entre ces arbres et nos derniers scrupules,
    Et, quittant tout portique et toutes colonnades,
    Transportés tout à coup par une sorte d'enthousiasme
        paisible

En faveur d'une vérité, aujourd'hui, qui soit verte,
Nous nous trouvions bientôt alités de tout notre long
   sur ce pré,
Dès longtemps préparé pour nous par la nature,
   —où n'avoir plus égard qu'au ciel bleu.

(21) L'oiseau qui le survole en sens inverse de l'écriture
Nous rappelle au concret, et sa contradiction,
Accentuant du pré la note différentielle
Quant à tels près ou prêt, et au prai de prairie,
Sonne brève et aiguë comme une déchirure
Dans le ciel trop serein des significations.
C'est qu'aussi bien, le lieu de la longue palabre
Peut devenir celui de la décision.

(22) Des deux pareils arrivés debout, l'un au moins,
Après un assaut croisé d'armes obliques,
Demeurera couché
D'abord dessus, puis dessous.

(23) Voici donc, sur ce pré, l'occasion, comme il faut,
Prématurément, d'en finir.

(24) Messieurs les typographes,
   Placez donc ici, je vous prie, le trait final.
   Puis, dessous, sans le moindre interligne, couchez mon
      nom,
   Pris dans le bas-de-casse, naturellement,
              Sauf les initiales, bien sûr,
              Puisque ce sont aussi celles
              Du Fenouil et de la Prêle
              Qui demain croîtront dessus.

Francis Ponge[32]

The first two stanzas, while setting the poem's apparently casual tone, introduce a continuum involving poet, reader, nature and text. The words "propose" and "disposés" immediately establish the relationship of equality and mutuality that obtains between us and nature, a relationship that "justement" subtly underscores. What automatically swells in our throats as we awaken to our experience of nature is a heavenly paean to the total integration of everything. Formulation accompanies awareness and joy reigns supreme.

The meadow has proposed itself in this fashion to the poet and he now wants to speak for it, to utter it. Accordingly, the meadow will *make* the poet's talk of today. By choosing "fera" over "sera" Ponge deftly eliminates whatever distance may separate his topic-thing from his text. Furthermore, with "propos" he both recalls "propose," along with that word's egalitarian resonance, and uses a term that means at once topic and utterance. Even the seemingly straightforward phrase "veux dire" is appropriately ambiguous, for while it expresses what the two words say literally, it also suggests, inevitably, the very common idiomatic sense of "vouloir dire." Thing, topic, utterance, and meaning will evidently merge in "Le Pré."

In the next three stanzas (three through five) Ponge rejects the notions that life and art are to be consumed or observed (i.e., simply "savored" or "appreciated"). Life for him is process and involvement while art is gesture and act, hence language, which is both symbolic and real action, is more capable of uttering or giving birth to the meadow than is painting.

So far, all is preparatory and anticipatory of birth and greenness (which itself prolongs the theme of genesis and growth). Both the text and the meadow, joined in an on-going symbiosis, are still in the earliest (pre-natal?) moments of coming into being, a stage that "Préparons" locates unequivocally. Henceforth, moreover, it will be as much a question of the meaning of "pré-" the prefix (along with some other meanings that [pre] can have) as of a meadow or of a text about a meadow.

But the second part of "Préparons" contains the verb "parer" which by itself can mean to prepare. Hence, the prefix "pré" is superfluous or pleonastic in the case of "préparer." Predictably, language as pleonasm or redundancy is an important theme of "Le Pré." The verb "parer" also means of course to adorn or embellish, which brings us to still another of the poem's themes, namely, rhetoric, the artificial manipulation of language for its own sake, language as pure figuration. For sometimes "Le Pré" seems to be simply the verbal (green) embellishment of the blank (brown) page.

Furthermore, "par," the radical of "parer," is at least as important to this poem as the monosyllable "pré." In fact, the particles "par" and "pré" will soon appear to be very closely related etymologically, a quasi-identification that will support in still another way the notion that the thing (the meadow) and its expression or embellishment (the text) are really one. The major role that "par" plays in "Le Pré" also gives rise to the suspicion that this text is an elaboration of "Fable," which, it will be recalled, focuses ultimately on its first word, "Par."

The next two stanzas (six and seven), among the other things they do, reinforce this suspicion, for suddenly we find ourselves starting the poem again. As in "Fable," the poet, even while moving forward, is drawn ever back to his opening statement. Every phrase he utters seems to require a second look, some explanatory comment. With his parenthetical explanation in stanza six, moreover, he re-introduces the theme of mutuality and interdependence between man and nature, a theme that the last line of this stanza, with its two optional versions, makes quite explicit. The hesitant, questioning and almost painfully self-conscious tone continues through stanza seven. "Mais," its first word, in fact, is one of Ponge's favorite pivots on which to swing about and re-examine what he has just said. (It will be recalled that "mais" performs this function in "Fable.") Here we are well into the poem and the poet is still poised, with us, "en surplomb sur la page," paralyzed by all sorts of scruples.

His "aphasia" becomes even more of an obsession with him in stanzas eight through ten. The interrogative phrase "Pourquoi donc," which opens and closes this section of the poem, sufficiently echoes "Parfois donc" to remind us that the poem has not really gotten under way yet. Within the frame of this twice-posed question the poem's "silence" is filled with rich details, some familiar and the others new. At the governing center of the first stanza in this group we find the phrase "Ce pré," in which the demonstrative adjective underscores the meadow-text's immediate and concrete presence. "Ce pré" is first compared to a handkerchief and then to a Persian rug, but in the lines immediately preceding this stanza it was, as earlier in the poem, a question of the page rather than the meadow. Thus, we have a series of well-modulated metamorphoses: a page becomes a handkerchief becomes a meadow becomes a rug.

But while a meadow is in some respects comparable to both a handkerchief and a Persian rug, it is essentially different from them, and what Ponge is trying to do here is to isolate the "qualité différentielle" of the meadow (as well as of the word-particle "pré"). Unlike the handkerchief or the rug, the meadow is "Fragile, mais non frangible," for when holes appear in it, it is simply that "La terre végétale y reprend parfois le dessus." By restoring to a figurative expression ("prendre le dessus") its literal application, the poet both amuses us and identifies a distinguishing characteristic of the meadow. As for the word-particle "pré," it too is "fragile, mais non frangible" since it can at times be dropped altogether with no apparent loss of meaning (as from the word "préparer") but never broken down or reduced any further than it already is.

The move away from the figurative and the abstractly analogical and toward the literal and the concrete makes Ponge's rare but precise use of the word "théorie" in stanza ten less surprising than it would otherwise be. What could be more abstract than a theory or more concrete than an advancing procession? No wonder the poet is still speechless—the materials with which he seeks to describe the meadow, the words, invariably call as much attention to themselves as they do to the meadow. Is "Le Pré" in fact concerned not so much with the meadow but with the limitations and real possibilities of language? The next two stanzas, eleven and twelve, would seem to require an affirmative answer to this question.

The Greek "naos," meaning the inner part of a temple or shrine, picks up the Greek-based "théorie" along with that word's sacred overtones. Knowing Ponge's predilection for neologisms and his great sensitivity to the malleability of words, we can also see in "naos," because of its context, hints of "chaos" and "néant." The mute procession has reached (note the choice of "*par*venus" over "arrivés") the innermost part or heart of what? Of chaos? Nothingness? Silence? Perhaps all three, for we have reached that place where words are redundant, where language is found in efficacious or modal gesture, as in a spinning prayer-wheel. The phrase "niveau logique" seems to refer to "logos," to that deep region, that root place, where, according to Ponge, things and their formulation are one. How appropriate, therefore, is the prayer-wheel, which expresses itself, quite literally makes prayers (persuasive speech par excellence), while it turns. But the poet quickly steps back from the perhaps too serious evocation of the prayer-wheel and again broaches the formal "subject" of his poem, the meadow, which he alludes to now, in wry fashion, as the "verticalités de l'endroit." This sudden and yet deft return to "le pré" paves the way for the poem's next five stanzas, thirteen through seventeen.

Instead of returning to the referent (the meadow), however, we have returned to the sign ("le pré") and to an explanation of its origins. Lines two and three of stanza thirteen begin, respectively, with "Près" and "Prêt," which in their slight phonic variation from "pré" make us conscious of that word's physicality, as did, in another way, the etymological explanation of the first line. But these lines also re-introduce the meadow by specifying its location and function. Line four, practically a leitmotif in the poem, continues the presence of the referent, while directly involving us ("nous") again.

The last line in stanza thirteen, probably the most compact in the whole poem, dwells solely on the sign. It starts out by breaking up the first word of the previous line, "Préparé," which is perhaps the single most important word in the poem, containing as it does "pré," "par," and "parer" (in its past participial form). But most importantly, line five recapitulates lines one through four. Its second word, "paré," is the French equivalent of the Latin *paratus*, so in a sense "pré" comes from "paré." Also, "paré" contracted ("Crase") would give "pré." Thus, the first three words of line five, if read as *pré* < *paré* > *pré*, constitute a recapitulation of line one. The last two words in line five pick up the first words of lines two and three respectively, while line five's last word, "prêt," is synonymous with the first word of line four ("Préparé") and in fact sums up all of line four rather succinctly. As we read line five, moreover, we notice that "pré," "près," and "prêt" are more similar to one another in the way they are actually pronounced than purists in matters of phonetics would have us believe, inasmuch as the [ɛ] in "près" and "prêt," being final, stressed and unchecked, tends to close toward [e].

The abyss of semantic and phonetic associations and reverberations we have entered seems bottomless. The poet has clearly placed the sign-referent "pré," the object of his loving attention, "en abîme" and has created a verbal machine as capable of giving us the meadow, in all of that object's density and ambiguity, as the meadow itself.

The "multiplication intérieure des rapports" continues through stanza fourteen. Its first line skillfully fuses sign and referent. Then, after being viewed as the past participle par excellence, "pré" is seen as the archetypal prefix, since it occurs in the word "préfixe" itself, as well as in the word "présent,"

which, significantly, comes from *prae esse* meaning to be before
or ahead. Now "pré" is at the head of (ahead of) "to be" in
"présent," and is present in "présent" before we notice it
there.

We conclude from the foregoing that if we look closely
enough at them, words are profoundly onomatopoetic, or at
least iconic, for they act out or mime what they mean. We
cannot escape our verbal roots, Ponge then declares, and we
should not try. "Ever backward and inward" would seem to be
his motto regarding language. We cannot lose our self-
consciousness as speakers, our constant awareness of the words
we utter, and that is for the best. Just as the spider's web, spun
out of his own substance, constitutes his "rayon d'action" and
gives the spider what mastery he has over his world (*GRP*, pp.
197-200), language for man, spun out of his substance, consti-
tutes his control, his consciousness, of the world. Words give
birth to consciousness by structuring the as yet unformulated.
We must get all the way back to our first words because there,
in the realm of *logos*, where onomatopoeia is the natural mode
of speech, we will find no gap between things and their expres-
sion, between referent and sign, between "l'objet" and the
"jeu de mots" that recreates "l'objet."

Fittingly enough, Ponge then restates, very concisely, his
theory of "l'objeu." He asserts that the variations on our origi-
nal utterances suffice to account for the intricate and grandiose
clockwork of the universe—provided of course that we utter all
the variations. While saying this, he gives us an example of
such a variation with the very pertinent verb "to speak."
"Paraboler" is certainly, at least hypothetically, a possible ear-
lier, hence more onomatopoetic, form of "parler." And if we
recall that "etymon" originally means "true," we are reminded
by Ponge that in an earlier version the verb to speak in French
may well have meant to speak in parables, to utter moral
truths. The case of "parler" and its origins seems to illustrate
Ponge's thesis that with regard to words, to penetrate their

opacity, to go into them and back with them through time we discover truth.

The preceding five stanzas (thirteen through seventeen), which constitute a kind of climax in "Le Pré," are followed by a full (horizontal) line of ellipses. The text then resumes, though for the time being at least the stanzaic form has yielded to plain prose. At the center of this typically self-conscious interpolation (which I call "stanza" eighteen), is the observation that the sign "pré" and the referent "pré" are similarly elemental in their respective domains. This same statement also exhibits the persistent presence of "par," both textually and in the key notion of means or agency. Grass comes into being thanks to the transformation of ashes by water, a metamorphosis that is a rebirth, a recycling of life's powers over death.

Immediately following the parenthetical prose passage and then another complete line of suspension points the stanzaic form of "Le Pré" resumes with a single line of verse: "L'orage originel a longuement parlé." The subject of the verse recalls "l'orage initial" from earlier in the poem and evokes, once again, the primordial or birth explosion to which Ponge refers in "Le Soleil placé en abîme."

After this line comes the poem's third and last full line of suspension points, which is followed by stanza twenty. Again the transition is smoothly modulated, this time with the repetition of "L'orage originel." As we move into stanza twenty we find once more a number of occurrences of "par" (in the word "par" itself, in "*par*tiellement," etc.). But the overall impression the stanza gives, for a while at least, is that finally something is about to happen or be said. At the end, however, we find the poet still mute, and in fact flat on his back on the meadow, gazing up at the sky.

Stanza twenty-one ends the poet's daydream rather abruptly. The bird flying across the meadow from right to left, opposite from the way in which we read and write, brings us, literally, to our senses, back to intractable reality, and is the agent by which the meadow-particle's specificity comes forth. "Pré" is an unsettling ripping sound in the impossibly quiet sky-mirror of word-meanings. Once we realize the intrusive, shaping nature of language, this place and occasion (i.e., this text) of preliminary talk, of palaver, can and does become the place of decision. The end of the poem becomes the beginning of awareness.

The next stanza, number twenty-two, is briefer than most of the others and also more puzzling, at least initially. Who or what are the "deux pareils" referred to in the first line? Now the whole poem seems to be concerned above all with language, both spoken and written, but especially spoken. Note, for example, in the previous stanza the word "palabre," which perfectly conveys the notion of the poem as pre-statement or preliminary talk. At the same time, "palabre" comes from "palabra," the Spanish for "parole," and both of these words derive from "parabolare," which also gives "parler." ("Parler" seems to turn up everywhere.) "Parole" and "palabre" are thus "pareils" in that they both come from the same Latin verb and because they have related meanings, even though one, "palabre," has a fairly restricted range of application. Compensating for this limitation, however, is the active situation in which "palabre" must always appear. In comparison, "parole" has lost much of its contact with actual speech, although it is still far more "alive" than "mot."

Two other words in stanza twenty-one are also linguistic "pareils," if in a slightly different way from "palabre" and "parole." This time both words appear in the text; they are "déchirure" and "décision." The radical of "déchirure" comes from the Frankish *skîran which means "to scratch," while the radical of "décision" comes from the Latin caedere which means "to cut." Of the two, only "déchirure" has kept and even increased its root force. "Décision" (which still meant "to slice" in the Latin decīdere) has been eviscerated in the war of words and has fallen into a figurative, abstract posture. "Déchirure"

alone remains vertical, vibrant with the power of its youth.
However, no regrets are expressed, nor would any be in order.
This is simply what happens. Words evolve in different ways,
some lose their concreteness earlier than others, while still
others joust with one another over some piece of semantic ter-
rain until one falls. But rarely is a fallen word truly lost, for
even horizontal and underground it can grow into something
else. By choosing "pareils" over "pairs" (which would have
been more appropriate to the "jousting" situation) Ponge
again utters the key particle "par," thereby integrates this
stanza into the poem and invites the kind of interpretation we
have just made.

The next two stanzas bring the poem to a close. As in "Fa-
ble," we are struck in stanza twenty-three by the absolute lit-
eralness of what is being said. Just as it does elsewhere in "Le
Pré," "donc" makes us pause and glance over our shoulder
even as we move forward. The phrase "sur ce pré" pinpoints
where we are—"en surplomb sur la page," overlooking *this*
meadow-text, which now, prematurely and yet fittingly, must
end. It will end just as "le pré" enters our consciousness
through formulation, through *this* formulation. For "Le Pré" is
a delivery or birth record, an account of the rise of something
out of nothing, out of chaos.

The typesetters are then addressed, for they are the agents,
the "pars," through whose (literal) labors "Le Pré" may exist as
a public document-place. The poet's request is most appropri-
ate: he asks them to place a (horizontal) line along the bottom
of his text and then to lay his name directly underneath. He
also asks that only his initials be in capitals because they are
also the initials of fennel and horsetail which tomorrow, after
his decline from concrete, specific and unique life into
abstract, generalized and common death, will break open the
soil declaring their form, their verticality above the horizontal
grave-meadow.

The key word-particles "pré" and "par" and the poem's key

word "parler" endure to the end. "Prêle" breaks down into
"prê" and "le" which, when reversed, are as close phonetically
to "le pré" as were "le près" and "le prêt." As for "par," the
capital letters F and P constitute "le paraphe" of Francis
Ponge. Abbreviated (after all, F and P are abbreviations for
Francis Ponge), "le paraphe" becomes "le par," and if *these* two
particles are reversed and joined (i.e., the precise opposite of
what was done with "Prêle") the result is "parle." What is
thrusting to the surface of the earth-brown page is speech.

Words exist in flux, in a state of semantic, phonetic and or-
thographic instability; they flow into and out of one another,
breaking up and forming new verbal units, with astonishing
ease. At the same time, language has an inner logic, an inter-
nal interconnectedness. The poet's role is to find these inter-
connections, to trace the patterns made by the shifting verbal
particles. Moreover, since language is consciousness, our
awareness of the world, hence since language coincides with
our world, to chart the domain of words is to change a maze
into a mansion, to make language what it potentially is al-
ready, man's self-created habitat. The spider makes his web
out of his own substance and then lives in it, the snail does the
same with his shell (*TP*, pp. 57-61), and man should do
likewise with his web-shell, language. This, among other
things, is what "Le Pré" is all about.

"Le Pré" is also the exploration of "par's" opacity that "Fa-
ble" suggests. In that sense the long, late poem picks up where
the brief, early poem leaves off and recapitulates everything
Ponge has done in between. If *Le Savon* builds up to and cul-
minates in a loving meditation on the word "avec,"[33] "Le Pré"
is a kind of *blason* on "par," or, more precisely, on "le par," the
phrase that ultimately jostles "le pré" out of the way to occupy
center stage by itself. Both "Fable" and "Le Pré" are about
speech. The word "fable" comes from the Latin *fari*, to speak,
while the phrase "le par," reversed and then joined, as we have
seen, forms "parle." If we reread the first line of "Fable"—"Par
le mot *par* commence donc ce texte"—we see even more links

now between it and "Le Pré" than we did before. Besides the obvious connections through "par" and "donc," we notice that the first two words of the line, when compressed, form "parle." We also note that the word "mot" in "Fable" is to "parole" in "Le Pré" what the phrase "ce texte" in the line in question is to "ce pré" in the later poem, and what the verb "commencer" in "Fable" is to "naître" in "Le Pré." In each case, "Le Pré" makes more concrete, more specific and more vital something already present in "Fable."

As we move from "Fable" to "Le Pré," we learn that language activated, that is, speech, is the agency, the means, "le par," by which consciousness is born. Without "fable" or "parle" all is randomness and chaos. The distinguishing faculty of man, his "note [or "qualité"] différentielle," is his word-making capacity. He alone can impose form on formlessness, life on death, genesis on entropy, endowed as he is with the power of formulation. He alone can parry ("parer") the thrust of the unformulated. This too is what "Le Pré" is all about.

The appeal and value of Ponge stem from the fact that he is truly a post-Existentialist poet. He assumes the absurd and goes beyond the despair that it inspires by refusing to dwell on the inevitable decline of everything and by rejoicing in the here and now, in his successive awakenings to the endless variety of the world. If Roquentin, Sartre's hero in *La Nausée*, is overwhelmed at that novel's climax by a vision of apocalyptic collapse, Ponge, throughout his *oeuvre*, celebrates the explosive rise of differentiation and definition, the birth of consciousness. And since consciousness and formulation are the same for Ponge, his poetry is of necessity metapoetic, turned in on itself, watching itself and guiding itself as it comes into being. What he says of Malherbe we must therefore say of him: "Il ne s'occupe que de son instrument."[34]

Unlike Malherbe, however, Ponge's abiding concern with his instrument, his implacable self-consciousness when writing, is both unabashed and central to his vision. In the middle of his long piece entitled "La Seine," he exclaims: "Confondons, confondons sans vergogne la Seine et le livre qu'elle doit devenir!" (*TP*, p. 557). If thing and text do merge in this case, the Seine will have entered our consciousness as a separate, living entity. If not, it will remain an abstraction, a crooked line on the map of France, a background feature of the Paris scene, or something so amorphous as to be non-existent in any concrete, delimited sense. Of course, only the right combination of vocables, only a spiral of words that somehow structures the maelstrom that the Seine opens up when it has been placed "en abîme," will bring the Seine into existence, carry it into our consciousness. For such a spiral to function, for it to become an "objeu," it will have to be metapoetic, ever attentive to itself, inasmuch as its terms are all and beneath them lies nothing but chaos.

For Ponge, the universe is a vast clockwork whose spinning wheels signify nothing beyond themselves. While he never mentions "l'analogie universelle" by name, his vision of an "horlogerie universelle" diametrically opposes Baudelaire's theory. His texts are not symbolic but literal, hence they are not poetic in a traditional way. Moreover, they speak neither of private obsessions nor of life's limitations, but instead seek merely to render widely differing cogs within our infinitely rich world. They aspire not to charm us but to immerse us in a total experience of the relative, of that which is at hand, and in so doing to revitalize our moribund capacity for sensuous reasoning. If the excesses of Symbolism and estheticism have contributed to our alienation from our proper place and function in the world, Ponge's metapoems help to reintegrate us into the world, for they demonstrate that the self is by nature participatory, intentional, that it is in a sense forever "out there" in that which it perceives and formulates. His achievement, one with profound consequences for contemporary man, is that he turns us back toward experience from the unbearable and false isolation of "pure" subjectivity.

III. René Char

René Char is a poet of special significance for this study. For an important five-year period in his early adult life one of Surrealism's principal exponents, he, like Reverdy, is an outstanding representative of the Orphic or means-oriented conception of poetry. Also, however, like Ponge, if less systematically and less radically, Char demonstrates or enacts in his practice the intentional thrust of perception. Furthermore, reflecting perhaps his compatibility with aspects of both Reverdy and Ponge, Char goes a long way toward synthesizing their conflicting responses to the phenomenon of entropy. Finally, and doubtless most pertinently for the present discussion, it was Char (along with Michel Leiris), and not Reverdy (d. 1960) or André Breton (d. 1966), who assured a direct link between, on the one hand, the original Dada-Surrealist group, including in this case Reverdy, and, on the other, *L'Ephémère* and *Argile*, possibly the most important manifestations of the continuing strength of the broad Surrealist current in French poetry to occur within the last ten years.

Surrealism, the movement that dominated French letters between the two World Wars, in one way or another seems to have touched virtually every major poet born since 1895 or shortly before. Reverdy, who was born in 1889, is a case in point. Slightly older than the original Surrealist triumvirate (André Breton, b. 1896, Philippe Soupault, b. 1897, Louis Aragon, b. 1897), he was already an established figure in avant-garde circles by 1924, the year in which Breton's epoch-making *Manifeste du surréalisme* first appeared. Nevertheless, in real if limited and mostly unintentional ways Reverdy participated in the rise of the new movement. As for Breton's near coeval, the fiercely independent Ponge (b. 1899), he sought out and mingled with the Surrealists for the better part of a year and was one of the signatories of the *Second manifeste du surréalisme* (1929). René Char, born in 1907, and perhaps the greatest French poet to emerge during the 1930's, also signed the *Second manifeste*. In addition, Char was an active member of the group from 1929 to 1934. The present chapter will focus on Char's work as it draws at least part of its sustenance from the Surrealist revolution in poetry, but more especially as this work explores and exploits, endlessly yet ever freshly, one of the central themes of Surrealism, the notion of contradiction.[1] But first of all I shall review very briefly the salient facts of Reverdy's and then Ponge's relations with the Surrealist group.

1. REVERDY, PONGE AND SURREALISM

Reverdy's first contact with the future Surrealists occurred in 1917-1918 when he published texts by Breton, Soupault and Aragon in his review *Nord-Sud*. Then between 1918 and 1920 he contributed to *Dada* and *Littérature* (first series), both proto-Surrealist organs, and in December 1924 his essay entitled "Le Rêveur parmi les murailles" appeared in the inaugural issue of *La Révolution surréaliste* (pp. 19-20). Breton for his part quotes and comments upon Reverdy's definition of the image in the first *Manifeste*,. where he also claims that "Reverdy est surréaliste chez lui."[2] While all of this might suggest a certain similarity of views between the two poets, in fact Reverdy kept his distance from Breton, in regard to whom he seems to have preferred the role of sometime editor or sympathetic if rather skeptical older friend to that of comrade-in-arms. In "Le Rêveur," for example, Reverdy expresses reservations about Breton's conception of Surrealism: "Je ne sais pas si le surréalisme doit être considéré comme une simple dictée automatique de la pensée. Pour moi je perds conscience de cette dictée dès qu'elle a lieu et, de plus, je ne sais encore d'où elle vient" (p. 19).

Furthermore, in October 1924, just two months before *La Révolution surréaliste* was launched, Yvan Goll brought out the first (and, as it turned out, only) issue of *Surréalisme*, a publication that contained, among other things, an avowedly Cubist-inspired manifesto (by Goll) and a poem by Reverdy. Against this background, the latter's connection with *La Révolution surréaliste* seems quite tenuous, for Reverdy contributed not a single poem to Breton's review during the five years of its existence and in fact published nothing at all in *La Révolution surréaliste* other than "Le Rêveur," an essay which in the end betokens broad moral support, not ideological agreement.

Reverdy's demurrals regarding Surrealism's "official" positions notwithstanding, his compatibility with at least some of the movement's aims and values seems undeniable. For example, even though he never participated in Surrealist experiments such as the *récits de rêve* and the *sommeils hypnotiques*, Reverdy is named, not without justification, by Aragon as one of the "Présidents de la République du rêve" in the latter's history of the role of the dream in the development of Surrealism.[3] Also, Reverdy's high esteem for the place of the marvelous in the grand scheme of things human, as evidenced by his assertion that "le propre de l'homme est son inexplicable besoin de merveilleux,"[4] equals that revealed by Breton in the first *Manifeste*: "Tranchons-en: le merveilleux est toujours beau, n'importe quel merveilleux est beau, il n'y a que le merveilleux qui soit beau."[5] But most indicative of Reverdy's kinship with an essential strain in Surrealism is his willingness to employ a term like "surréalité" in the course of articulating his belief that art's function is to take us to another, deeper, less verifiable, more hazardous, realm of feeling:

> Ce qu'on appelle réalité en art c'est un ensemble de rapports dont la justesse parvient à nous donner une image vive et susceptible de provoquer une émotion plus intense et surtout plus constante que le vrai. Par le rapprochement des

choses par leurs rapports les plus lointains, en apparence
même inexistants, on arrive à la surréalité. L'émotion, par
ces moyens obtenue, est plus subjective, plus profonde, in-
finiment plus rare aussi. Elle échappe davantage à la con-
frontation au dehors—à tout contrôle. Elle est plus précaire.
Le concours de circonstances qu'elle implique est plus
héroïque, c'est-à-dire beaucoup plus hasardeux.[6]

Somewhat ironically, Ponge, though at one point in his life
formally a part of the Surrealist group, probably stayed even
more aloof from it than Reverdy, who never joined the move-
ment. Ponge has explained his reasons for openly allying him-
self with the group at a particular moment in time (in 1929) as
follows:

> J'ai fait acte d'adhésion au groupe surréaliste. . . . exacte-
> ment au moment où ce groupe a commencé à connaître des
> schismes très importants . . . lorsque toute la presse,
> naturellement presse bourgeoise, disait: "C'en est fini, nous
> sommes bien contents, voilà les gens de talent qui s'en vont
> de là." . . . C'est dans cette conjoncture que j'ai fait adhé-
> sion physique au groupe, c'est-à-dire que je suis allé au 42
> rue Fontaine, chez Breton, et au *Cyrano* qui était le café où
> ils se réunissaient à ce moment-là. J'ai fait ça pendant un
> peu moins d'un an. . . . j'ai adhéré, j'ai signé le manifeste
> qui annonçait le *Surréalisme au Service de la Révolution*. C'était
> donc exactement au moment de la mutation, si vous voulez,
> au commencement de ce qu'on appelle, dans les manuels de
> littérature, actuellement, ou d'histoire littéraire, la seconde
> époque du surréalisme. C'était le moment de sa politisa-
> tion.[7]

Thus it would appear that Ponge supported the Surrealists
when he did in order to express publicly his solidarity with
them at a critical juncture in their existence. What Reverdy
had done if only obliquely in 1924 presumably out of friend-

ship, Ponge did rather flamboyantly five years later out of a sense of political commitment.

Ponge steered clear of Surrealism (except for this brief period in 1929) in part no doubt because he too, like Reverdy, simply could not bring himself to practice automatic writing or to believe in its value.[8] Furthermore, as Michel Beaujour has pointed out, with their enormous stress on inspiration, the Surrealists in effect denied the productive process in writing.[9] In so doing they assumed exactly the kind of naive stance vis-à-vis their own scriptural activity that would inevitably clash with Ponge's highly self-conscious approach to the production of texts. Finally, as Philippe Sollers has noted in his conversations with Ponge, "l'accent est mis toujours, dans l'idéologie surréaliste, sur le rêve, l'imagination, le merveilleux."[10] This aspect especially of Surrealism has had, in the words of Beaujour, "deplorable ideological consequences since it opened up the door to occultism and mysticism."[11] It is precisely such tendencies within contemporary literature that Ponge has resisted throughout his life.

2. SURREALISM AND CHAR

Unlike Reverdy and Ponge, Char frequented the Surrealists at a potentially crucial stage in his development, between the ages of twenty-two and twenty-seven. For this reason alone one might be tempted to liken his sojourn among the Surrealists to Reverdy's formative stint with the Cubists. In both cases a young *méridional* of poetic genius spent his first years in Paris in the company of the most advanced creators of his day. But the similarity stops there. Reverdy's early Paris period was, according to his own account, a kind of apprenticeship: "De 1910 à 1914 j'ai reçu la leçon des cubistes. Ces tableaux si dépouillés, si simples. . . . J'ai eu l'ambition d'obtenir cela en littérature."[12] Also, prior to arriving in the capital he had apparently made no serious attempt at writing poetry. Char, on the other hand, had been writing poetry since 1923, and he published his first two collections, *Les Cloches sur le coeur* (1928) and *Arsenal* (1929), before meeting the Surrealists or even leaving the Midi. Logically, then, Surrealism simply could not have had the same impact on Char in 1929-1934 that Cubism had had on Reverdy two decades earlier.[13]

More than one critic has contended that Char's involvement with the Surrealists seems to have been more of a liberating or catalyzing experience than a shaping one. In effect, such critics maintain, Char's Surrealist phase provided him with an opportunity for further experimentation and growth within an essentially formed poetic identity. Virginia La Charité, for example, has argued, persuasively in my view, that "Char's ultimate poetic vision appears before his participation in the Surrealist movement."[14] She also points out that the three basic forms Char has utilized—the prose poem, the free verse poem and the poetic aphorism—are modes he had practiced before allying himself with Breton and company. La Charité lists the major themes of Char's writings, from his pre-Surrealist period onward, as follows: "discovery of the real, need for freedom, love as a condition for poetry, fusion of opposites into one entity or totality" (p. 39). That such themes should inform his earliest writings suggests, among other things, that by 1929 Char was ripe for seduction by the revolutionary, transrational enterprise that Breton and his cohorts were embarked upon.

Surrealism, it will be recalled, seeks above all to end man's alienation from the deepest roots of his being. In the first manifesto, Breton proposes to unlock, by means of psychic automatism, the real functioning of thought "en l'absence de tout contrôle exercé par la raison, en dehors de toute préoccupation esthétique ou morale." This enterprise "repose sur la croyance à la réalité supérieure de certaines formes d'association négligées jusqu'à lui, à la toute-puissance du rêve, au jeu désintéressé de la pensée,"[15] and it would put man in touch once again, and at will, with his unconscious mind through

automatic writing, dream recitals, self-induced hallucinatory
states and various forms of verbal game-playing. In short, Sur-
realism would open up the entire realm of the imagination, so
as to create, in Sarane Alexandrian's words, "un monde où le
rêve serait le frère de l'action, et non un simple démenti du
réel."[16]

Char's alliance with the Surrealists was for a time quite
complete. Between 1930 and 1934 he published no fewer than
three works under the imprint of the Editions Surréalistes, as
well as *Ralentir travaux*, a collective effort written in collabora-
tion with Breton and Paul Eluard. Both La Charité and
Georges Mounin consider *Artine* (1930), Char's first text pub-
lished by the Editions Surréalistes and dedicated to Breton, as
perhaps the most classically Surrealist of his writings of this
period. Reading *Artine*, one has to agree with Mounin when he
asserts that "dans sa substance, *Artine* . . . offre la plus parfaite
orthodoxie surréaliste," that it is an "exaltation d'abord des
pouvoirs du sommeil et du rêve."[17] The poem's opening para-
graph sets the scene, so to speak, for the rest of this anti-
realistic but not unrepresentational text, a text that makes one
think of Salvador Dali's paintings of roughly the same period
(Dali, it might be remembered, also signed the second man-
ifesto of Surrealism):

> *Dans le lit qu'on m'avait préparé il y avait: un animal san-
> guinolent et meurtri, de la taille d'une brioche, un tuyau de plomb,
> une rafale de vent, un coquillage glacé, une cartouche tirée, deux
> doigts d'un gant, une tache d'huile; il n'y avait pas de porte de
> prison, il avait le goût de l'amertume, un diamant de vitrier, un
> cheveu, un jour, une chaise cassée, un ver à soie, l'objet volé, une
> chaîne de pardessus, une mouche verte apprivoisée, une branche de
> corail, un clou de cordonnier, une roue d'omnibus.*[18]

As La Charité has observed (p. 49), a Surrealist dislocation of
objects has occurred here; those listed are bizarre to the point
of fanciful, completely heterogeneous and thus thoroughly

incongruous in their relationship to one another. On the referential level, all logical linkage or sequence among the objects is disrupted, despite the traditional, even fluent, character of the sentence's syntax (in sharp contrast, it might be noted, to the broken syntax of Reverdy's verse poetry, where external reference carries the burden of coherence). But the compilation succeeds in establishing the strange atmosphere of dream that hovers over the rest of the poem.

Both Mounin (p. 104) and La Charité (p. 53) interpret the concluding sentence of *Artine*—"Le poète a tué son modèle"—as Char's repudiation of Surrealism's rather exclusive emphasis in poetic composition on "le rêve et l'inconscient et l'irréel."[19] As Mounin further observes in this connection: "Fidèle à sa passion héraclitéenne pour l'affrontement conscient des contraires, [Char] se refuse à résoudre l'antinomie raison-déraison par la négation du premier terme" (p. 105). More recently, Sarane Alexandrian has proposed "Eaux-mères," from *Abondance viendra* (1932-1933), as the text in which "Char annonce qu'il va changer de mode de vie et de manière d'écrire. . . . Il n'accepte plus sans contrôle ce qui vient, il y choisit des éléments qu'il met à des places rigoureusement déterminées de l'édifice à construire."[20] While they may differ as to which poem from Char's Surrealist period marks his break with the movement, in their general approach to the question of the poet's attitude toward the role of reason, choice and will in poetic composition, Mounin and Alexandrian agree. Their judgment in this regard finds support in a later utterance by Char himself, a remark which, it is worth pointing out, would place the poet closer to Reverdy than to Breton: "Le poète doit tenir la balance égale entre le monde physique de la veille et l'aisance redoutable du sommeil."[21]

In a general sense Surrealism seems to have given Char encouragement to pursue goals he had set for himself prior to 1929. More specifically, it would appear to have moved him to open himself up to all the levels of his consciousness and to use all the words at his command combined in every way possible.[22] Finally, and most instructively for the present context, Surrealism probably inspired Char to plunge ever more deeply into contradiction as a potential source of truth.

A number of twentieth-century thinkers, including the Surrealists, have reached the conclusion that one way to escape Western man's traditional sense of logic, as well as the hegemony of rationalism, is to go back beyond Plato and Aristotle to those theorists of contradiction, the pre-Socratic philosophers. Heidegger is perhaps the most illustrious of contemporary "rediscoverers" of Heraclitus and others.[23] Breton on several occasions remarked on the great impact Heraclitus had upon his own intellectual development.[24] Ponge has also spoken admiringly of the pre-Socratics, as did Camus.[25] For all of them, the fundamental difference between Aristotle and Heraclitus resides in the latter's validation of the notion of contradiction which (unlike the principle of identity that has founded Western thought since Aristotle) in turn validates the dialectical process. Tristan Tzara, founder of Dada, one-time colleague of Breton on *Littérature* and, along with Char and others, signer of the *Second manifeste du surréalisme*, concludes his 1918 *Manifeste dada* with this flourish: "DADA DADA DADA, hurlements des douleurs crispées, entrelacements des contraires et de toutes les contradictions, des grotesques, des inconséquences: LA VIE."[26] More fully than anyone else in what might be called the Dada-Surrealist group, René Char, who explicitly relates his obsession with contradiction to his admiration for Heraclitus, realizes in his practice Tzara's theoretical equation of contradiction and life.

In France, as we are seeing once again, this time involving Char and Heraclitus, poetry and philosophy often tend to merge. Char's affinities with two other philosophical thinkers, his contemporaries Heidegger and Camus, are in their own way just as real. Furthermore, a fusion of poetry and philosophy also occurs in Heidegger, who derived at least a part of his philosophy from Hölderlin.[27] We have seen how a philosophical essay by Camus can clarify the endeavors of two ex-

tremely different poets, Reverdy and Ponge. Char, far more
completely than Reverdy (to say nothing of Ponge), inhabits
the same spiritual realm as Camus, and perhaps as Heidegger
too, inasmuch as Char was the philosopher's favorite French
poet.[28] Camus, another admirer of Char, felt a profound kin-
ship with the poet, a feeling that was reciprocated.[29] Thus it is
hardly surprising that for Char, as for Reverdy and Ponge,
Camus provides an illuminating reference point. In the case of
Char, however, it is not so much a single work (Le Mythe de
Sisyphe) that sheds light on his oeuvre as it is the entire Camus
canon. A moral fervor analogous to the one that pervades
Camus's writings colors Char's oeuvre. Both writers search
above all for human dignity amidst the absurdity of life. In
their contained urgency, Camus's stories and essays especially
recall Char's poetic aphorisms, those lapidary, oracular
maxims which, like Reverdy's, are alternately about art—
poetry in particular—and life. Char's aphorisms, however, are
usually more concrete than Reverdy's, less removed from
poetry itself, and in that sense closer to Ponge's pronounce-
ments on art and poetry. Indeed, those Char aphorisms that
deal with art and poetry frequently achieve the perfect blend of
thought and feeling, method and adventure, that characterizes
the very best poésie critique. But whether esthetic or ethical in
orientation, Char's aphorisms generally marry poetry to phi-
losophy within a framework of contradiction in a way that is
remarkably reminiscent of Heraclitus:

> Il nous faut une haleine à casser des vitres. Et pourtant il
> nous faut une haleine que nous puissions retenir long-
> temps.[30]

3. POET OF CONTRADICTION

With few exceptions, René Char's poems start out at a high
pitch of intensity which is rarely relaxed and in fact usually

increases. Char, moreover, maintains his extremely tense, vig-
orous style at least as consistently in his prose poetry as he does
in his verse poems. That this should be so is quite remarkable
given the inherently discursive, muting tendency of prose as
compared with the more paratactic possibilities of verse, hence
the greater potential of verse for dramatic, polarized juxtaposi-
tion. Because of the tension that obtains between the eruptive
texture of his poems and the smooth prose vehicle that he often
chooses, Char seems both more impressive and more authenti-
cally himself as a prose poet than as a poet in verse. In either
form, however, his unfailing capacity to energize to the ut-
most degree the individual words and phrases of what are in
the end thoroughly organized structures suggests that a con-
vulsive paradox throbs at the heart of his poetry, that in Char
the forces of total anarchy, if not utter destruction, are con-
stantly at war with those of complete control, absolute order.

The striking incongruity between texture and structure in
Char, while it is doubtless responsible for the almost palpable
vitality that his texts possess, also reflects the poet's abiding
commitment to the principle of contradiction. Char rejects one
of the fundamental premises of Western thought, Aristotle's
principle of identity (a thing cannot at the same time be itself
and something else), in favor of the belief in the identity of
opposites espoused by Heraclitus, whom Char admires enor-
mously.[31] Nevertheless, despite the convergence of views be-
tween Char and Heraclitus in this most basic area and despite
Char's growing predilection over the years for a Sibylline,
Heraclitus-like aphorism, the unique qualities of Char's
poetry, especially his prose poetry, would scarcely emerge
from a comparison of that poetry with the pre-Socratic's fa-
mous fragments. On the other hand, because of their profound
philosophical affinity, linking the two men's names does con-
stitute a useful point of departure for a determination of Char's
specificity as a poet.

Char's adherence to Heraclitean contradiction is felt

throughout his *oeuvre*, from titles of collections through poetic
technique to the deepest level of vision. The title of one of his
plaquettes, for example, joins two semantically opposed but
phonically similar nouns, *L'Effroi la joie* (Saint Paul: Au Vent
d'Arles, 1969), a coupling that sums up, very succinctly,
Char's whole quickened, apparently ambivalent, yet ulti-
mately affirmative, response to life. "Commune présence," a
poem of major importance for Char and a relatively early text
(1936), comprises a number of paired contraries that shed
light on both his technique and his vision. Its last eight lines
are particularly significant in this regard:

> Tu as été créé pour des moments peu communs
> Modifie-toi disparais sans regret
> Au gré de la rigueur suave
> Quartier suivant quartier la liquidation du monde se
>   poursuit
> Sans interruption
> Sans égarement
>
> Essaime la poussière
> Nul ne décèlera votre union.[32]

In tone and substance the first two lines contradict each other.
After a gentle exhortation in which the poet informs someone,
doubtless himself, that he must be ready to rise to exceptional
occasions, he then says, in effect, 'Adjust and fade away with-
out a murmur.' Line three completes the sense of line two and
resolves or at least recognizes the conflict between that line and
the first. The key phrase here, virtually a contradiction in
terms, is "rigueur suave," whose first word captures the es-
sence of line one, while "suave" picks up line two. Like the
title *L'Effroi la joie*, the phrase "rigueur suave" exemplifies one
of Char's basic techniques, that of juxtaposing semantically in-
compatible words for a specific effect. The phrase also conveys,
in its context, Char's attitude toward life, which seems to be

an unsynthesized combination of total resistance and total acceptance. The surface tension he creates by lining up mutually exclusive terms is thus mirrored at the poem's depth, where Char's fundamental, paradoxical stance is adumbrated.

The next three lines also contain a contradiction, if in a slightly less obvious way than the first three lines. The fourth and fifth lines quickly present the entropic view of the world's destiny that haunts so many twentieth-century writers (not least, as we have seen, Reverdy and, by rejection, Ponge). But Char's variation on this deeply pessimistic theme comes with line six, which both parallels line five and diverges from it drastically. The final decline of all and everything into formlessness is already in progress and it is relentless, but that does not or at least should not create *égarement*, inner disorder. The inevitability of cosmic chaos need not undo spiritual order. The lines "Sans interruption/Sans égarement" thus embody a contradiction that is not unlike those contained in the phrases "rigueur suave" and "fright joy."

The last two lines of "Commune présence" are set off from the rest, and rightly so because they contain a climactic command—"Essaime la poussière"—and its reward if heeded—"Nul ne décèlera votre union." With the first of these lines we have yet another contradiction in terms; a swarm of bees and a cloud of dust are only visually analogous (just as *l'effroi* and *la joie* are only phonically similar). In essence they are contraries, the one suggesting fragments vitalized, unified, about to move up and away, and the other connoting destructive explosion followed by drift into ever greater dispersion and eventual nothingness. The injunction and its promise assert that the final, centerless settling of the particles is not to be denied but seized and turned into a swarm, and that if this is accomplished a state of at-oneness with the world will be attained. Once again by establishing a verbal polarity the poet reveals his moral vision. In terse, elliptical and imperious language he enjoins his listener (himself and now his reader too?)

to accept the fact of entropy but to resist the inner paralysis that can accompany such lucidity.

"Les Premiers Instants," a prose poem belonging to a group entitled *La Fontaine narrative* (1947), typifies Char's poetry in ways that take us up to and beyond Heraclitus, to what Char refers to elsewhere as "l'exaltante alliance des contraires."[33] But even before we read the poem, we see in the group title an internal contradiction characteristic of Char. For a fountain, even as it arcs into being also and at every instant disappears, its myriad droplets resembling so many scattering specks of dust. But the adjective "narrative" gives this fountain's perpetual disintegration a form that saves it, that of duration and continuity. The bead-droplets are as strung out on a rosary and told, narrated. Here, as in the case of the rising swarm, a violent burst or explosion is held together, a split second of perception prolonged. What at first seemed the inappropriate union of discordant terms ("fontaine" and "narrative") now appears as a truly exalting alliance of contraries.

The text of "Les Premiers Instants" offers similar harmonious discords:

> Nous regardions couler devant nous l'eau grandissante. Elle effaçait d'un coup la montagne, se chassant de ses flancs maternels. Ce n'était pas un torrent qui s'offrait à son destin mais une bête ineffable dont nous devenions la parole et la substance. Elle nous tenait amoureux sur l'arc tout-puissant de son imagination. Quelle intervention eût pu nous contraindre? La modicité quotidienne avait fui, le sang jeté était rendu à sa chaleur. Adoptés par l'ouvert, poncés jusqu'à l'invisible, nous étions une victoire qui ne prendrait jamais fin.[34]

Note, for example, the dominant use of the imperfect tense, which, by encasing the poem in a prime mode of anecdote, opposes and hence to a degree mitigates its urgent tone. And it is precisely the insistent, barely controlled immediacy of "Les Premiers Instants" that identifies it as Char's.

But how exactly does the poet achieve the effect of "tensed serenity"? To answer this question we must take note of the act or event that the poem records. In a sense, the entire text is devoted to defining its first word, "Nous." Paradoxically, it accomplishes this task not through delimitation or exclusion, the usual methods of definition, but by a gesture of opening up, of inclusion. The self (already expanded somewhat by the choice of "Nous" over "Je") is rapidly and thoroughly effaced as a subject that stands apart from and gazes upon a scene as object. Rather, it is invaded and given identity by a series of ineffable perceptions, which it nonetheless formulates and in so doing endows with existence. Subject and object thus create each other through a fruitful dialectic.

Diction, together with the poem's flowing and yet breathless rhythm, contributes immeasurably to the highly charged character of the dialectic. The last word in the first sentence, "grandissante," raises that sentence to the tauter level of the second, where the phrase "d'un coup" accentuates the already emphatic "effaçait" and where "se chassant" particularizes and vivifies "couler" of sentence one. In the next two sentences the phrases "bête ineffable," "tenait amoureux" and "l'arc tout-puissant" continue and increase the intensification. The "first instants" clearly are among those "moments peu communs" to which the poet refers in "Commune présence," one of those privileged, "matinal" times from which ordinariness and moderateness have been eradicated, in which the warmth of life itself has been restored to spilled blood, where destructive explosion has somehow been harnessed for good, pulverization redeemed and made a victory without end.

As it moves from its first word to its last, Char's poem dramatizes phenomenology's notion of intentionality. Perceiver and perceived fit into an overarching scheme that both exceeds them and permits the experience of *dévoilement*, the unveiling of being, to occur. For the "subject" in this case ("Nous") exists only to the extent that it is annihilated as a private, closed entity and reborn in each and every one of its "objects," where it finds its only real delineation. Also, for Char poetry and truth are synonymous,[35] while an individual poem is "lumière, apport de l'être à la vie."[36] What "Les Premiers Instants" shows us is that poetry can be the means by which we lose our separate selves and accede to the fullness of being, to truth, a design for poetry Char theorizes about in "Le Rempart des brindilles":

> Le dessein de la poésie étant de nous rendre souverain en nous impersonnalisant, nous touchons, grâce au poème, à la plénitude de ce qui n'était qu'esquissé ou déformé par les vantardises de l'individu.[37]

Thus, like Eliot and unlike poets locked inside the Romantic tradition, Char believes, not unparadoxically, in impersonality as the proper goal of poetry, as the road to sovereignty, to a selfhood beyond egoism. As Char's theory and practice make abundantly clear, poetry for him is a means, not an end in itself, an activity through whose accomplishment the poet steps out of himself and, once again in the words of Wallace Stevens, "barefoot into reality."

"Front de la rose," a poem from the same group of texts as Char's assertion of the "impersonalizing" design of poetry, *Poèmes des deux années* (1955), brings us still nearer to the heart of his vision:

> Malgré la fenêtre ouverte dans la chambre au long congé, l'arôme de la rose reste lié au souffle qui fut lá. Nous sommes une fois encore sans expérience antérieure, nouveaux venus, épris. La rose! Le champ de ses allées éventerait même la hardiesse de la mort. Nulle grille qui s'oppose. Le désir resurgit, mal de nos fronts évaporés.
>
> Celui qui marche sur la terre des pluies n'a rien à redouter de l'épine, dans les lieux finis ou hostiles. Mais s'il s'arrête et se recueille, malheur à lui! Blessé au vif, il vole en cendres, archer repris par la beauté.[38]

As in the case of the much admired "Congé au vent," which this text recalls, time, in a way peculiar to Char alone perhaps, is suspended, the present instant isolated. What is specifically lopped off is the past, and we are totally at one with our immediate perception of the rose. But present time in Char, if it obliterates past time, always implies future time, or, more precisely, a leaning or a straining toward the unexpected, not-yet-ordered gift of the unknown, toward "l'inespéré."[39] Also, Char's present is not stillness but movement, not concentration of the self in frozen recollection but headlong dispersion of the self throughout the endless pathways of experience, be they rosy or thorny, wild or tamed.

Essentially "Front de la rose" is constructed along bipartite and contrastive lines, with its first paragraph consisting of primarily "positive" matter and the second predominantly "negative." The most obvious (but by no means only) indication of this formal division is the occurrence of "rose" (twice) in paragraph one and of "épine" in paragraph two. More pervasively, there is the miracle of openness and time suspended in the first paragraph, while the terrible risk entailed by an ingathering of the self dominates the second paragraph. Yet this structural breakdown is only roughly accurate since each paragraph has elements and attributes of the other. For example, "mort" and "mal" darken the generally limpid first paragraph, while terminal "beauté" retrospectively brightens the second.

As for textural features, "Front de la rose" begins in leisurely and fairly conventional fashion, but by the end of the second sentence things have tightened up considerably and thenceforth the choice of words and the pace are unmistakably Char's. Compacted into a rapid sequence of assertive and relatively simple statements is that now familiar decisive and imperious diction that contests the serene prose form: "éventerait," "hardiesse," "mort," "Nulle grille," "s'oppose," "désir," "resurgit," "mal," "fronts évaporés." The last phrase in this series ("fronts évaporés"), with its partial echo of the title, lets us see what is happening in the poem: the rose with its "front" and the "champ de ses allées" literally supplants "nous" and "nos fronts évaporés." Consciousness is at best only readiness, "désir"; of itself it is nothing since it depends for its very existence on that of which it is conscious. As in "Les Premiers Instants," subject attains being only in its object; our foreheads are evaporated by, that is, exchanged for and realized by, the surface or face and the depth or intricacy of the rose.

The tone of the second paragraph is appreciably more violent than that of the first, even though its opening statement retains something of the deliberate rhythm of paragraph one's topic sentence. On the other hand, its stark, somber vocabulary is fully in keeping with the rest of paragraph two. The phrase "il vole en cendres" stamps the passage as Char's. Because of the idiomatic expression "voler en éclats," we expect to find "éclats" in place of "cendres," and because of our expectations we in a sense do, so little is the residual thrust of the cliché parried by Char's variant form. That we *feel* "éclats" under "cendres" tends to assimilate the image to Char's obsession with explosion and thus make the image familiar to us. At the same time, the word "cendres" contributes far more to the unity and density of the poem than "éclats" ever could. A reddish glow, introduced by the rose and reinforced by resurgent desire, suffuses the text. The ashes focus this glow even as they scatter it to the four winds, showing what deadly dispersal ensues, paradoxically, when the self tries to contract, to fold back on itself. The archer who stops in his tracks instead of striding on is destroyed by the very prey he would capture, beauty, which like poetry and truth is synonymous for Char with being-that-is-about-to-be-disclosed:

> Dans nos ténèbres, il n'y a pas une place pour la Beauté. Toute la place est pour la Beauté.[40]

This cryptic aphorism, which, significantly, concludes Char's "Resistance Diary" ("Feuillets d'Hypnos"), is glossed by—and in turn glosses—"Front de la rose," which also ends on and in beauty. Beauty-being is that which will flood "nos ténèbres" with the light of perception; it is that all-encompassing state in and for which disclosure occurs. Darkness and ignorance are simply unrealized light and awareness, hence "ténèbres," or readiness for poetic illumination, and "lumière," the informing light of the poem, are in a sense not opposite but identical.

In Char's poetic universe the true opposite of light, especially sunlight, is rain.[41] But here too the polarity is unstable. In "Front de la rose," for example, the walking figure at the beginning of paragraph two, a positive presence in Char, goes far toward neutralizing the menacing associations of "sur la terre des pluies." The title of a more recent collection by Char offers an even more striking case of harmonious discord involving rain: *Dans la pluie giboyeuse* (Gallimard, 1968). A cloud bursts thereby losing its once great height and unity. Rainfall as centerless settling diametrically opposes the image of the rising swarm that is central to Char's poetry.[42] But by modifying his noun with "giboyeuse" the poet counterbalances the negative weight of "pluie." To be in the game-rich rain is perhaps not such an unhappy fate after all.

One prose poem in *Dans la pluie giboyeuse* has an exceptionally high density of subtly interwoven and revelatory contradictions. The poem's title alone, "Bienvenue," strongly hints that a heightened, future-oriented moment has been reached, the importance of which eclipses all past time or at least relegates it to a purely waiting or prefatory status. As in the case of "Les Premiers Instants" and "Front de la rose," the present instant, cut off from what has been and turned toward what is to come, will in all likelihood focus on itself.

The text of "Bienvenue," with its series of interlocking contraries, both stated and implied, is like a page out of a ledger, so explicitly does it establish "credit" and "debit" columns:

Ah! que tu retournes à ton désordre, et le monde au sien. L'asymétrie est jouvence. On ne garde l'ordre que le temps d'en haïr l'état de pire. Alors en toi s'excitera le désir de l'avenir, et chaque barreau de ton échelle inoccupée et tous les traits refoulés de ton essor te porteront, t'élèveront d'un même sentiment joyeux. Fils de l'ode fervente, tu abjureras la gigantesque moisissure. Les solstices fixent la douleur diffuse en un dur joyau diamantin. L'enfer à leur mesure que les râpeurs de métaux s'étaient taillé, redescendra vaincu dans son abîme. Devant l'oubli nouveau, le seul nuage au ciel sera le soleil.

   Mentons en espoir à ceux qui nous mentent: que l'immortalité inscrite soit à la fois la pierre et la leçon. (p. 34)

The poem's basic conflict involves order and disorder, with Char clearly favoring the latter. Under the rubric of disorder we find lack of symmetry, youth, future orientation, rising flight, joy, a fervent ode, forgetfulness and the sun, while under that of order we see hatred, gigantic rot, hard fixity, reductive shaping, descent into the abyss of hell and, by implication, the past. Though totally schematic, this two-way breakdown does not fundamentally misrepresent "Bienvenue," which seems to dramatize Char's own admission that "l'obsession de la moisson et l'indifférence à l'Histoire sont les deux extrémités de mon arc."[43] The poet would rather harvest the peak of the here and now than mold what has gone by into History.

   "Bienvenue" ends as it begins, with a hortatory command. But now it is wished that concrete and abstract, material and moral, merge, that written immortality (the fervent ode?) be both the stone in which it is inscribed and the lesson it conveys. Yet leading into and undermining whatever optimism the wish may generate is the implicit avowal of a total context of falsehood, a global war of lies: "Mentons en espoir à ceux qui nous mentent." On examining these words closely, however, we note that the symmetry between liar and liar is not perfect. The phrase "en espoir" destroys the statement's balance and dilutes its pessimism by introducing, literally, the element of hope, hope that a lie will become a truth, that contradictions will cease to exist as such, that order and disorder will become one and the same.

The vitalizing imbalance that the phrase "en espoir" injects into an otherwise perfectly balanced statement actualizes the poem's second sentence: "L'asymétrie est jouvence." This brief remark, moreover, provides us with a major key to Char's poetry. His contradictions, never balanced, always gravitating toward identity, have a dynamism, an electric élan, as if they did indeed spring from "la fontaine de jouvence." Char's present, for example, stands between past and future, but it pulsates precisely because it lists in the direction of the future, because of an imbalance without which there would be only stasis, paralysis.

The first sentence in "Bienvenue" also resonates far beyond its immediate context: "Ah! que tu retournes à ton désordre, et le monde au sien." Char, we now see, begins this poem the way he ends "Commune présence," accepting entropy as the inevitable fate of all and everything. At the same time, however, and again as he does in the closing lines of "Commune présence," the poet transforms that dreadful knowledge into something positive. This is the contextual function of the second sentence. In fact, the statement "L'asymétrie est jouvence," thanks to its position, contributes even more to the poem than its sweeping proposition alone would suggest. As the subject of the poem's second sentence, lack of symmetry stretches semantically to include lack of form, whence it follows that chaos and total amorphousness constitute not a last end but a "jouvence," a source of life, of new and more open forms.

Char's most recent collection of poems, the forty-four-page *Aromates chasseurs* (Paris: Gallimard, 1975), thematizes entropy and the notion of contradiction in ways that are by now quite familiar to us. In other respects, too, the poet's latest work is of a piece with his previous production. Anti-rational, Surrealistic touches persist: e.g., "Le train disparu, la gare part en riant à la recherche du voyageur" (p. 23). A moralistic strain runs through this collection as it did earlier ones, and the image of the archipelago that haunts Char's *oeuvre* dominates the first poem, entitled "Evadé d'archipel," and turns up elsewhere in the *plaquette* either as such or in transposed form. Georges Blin's interpretation of this image, formulated more than a dozen years ago, is as pertinent today as it was then:

> L'image de l'archipel se formait dans cette oeuvre bien avant que Char ne l'eût relevée pour programme. Archipel surtout grec, cela va sans dire: le mot ne signifie pas pour rien mer principale. L'Hellade, vue comme une "chaîne de volcans," telle que nous l'a faite le déluge de Zeus, pour la survie d'un roi, lui aussi semeur de pierres. Ces blocs, vertèbres de l'étendue, ce sont les irréductibles témoins d'une intégrité qui ne combat que par flots, non débris, mais "brisants"; briseurs d'horizons. Ils doivent à l'érosion de ne plus la craindre.[44]

The archipelago seems the perfect image for Char to use in order to express his oxymoric vision since, as Blin suggests, it conveys the contradictory notion of diaspora (on the surface) and unity (at the depths), as well as a trans-entropic or post-Apocalyptic view. That Char understood at some point along the way the enormous potential of this image for his work seems undeniable (witness his collection *La Parole en archipel*) and, what is more important, that he was able thenceforth systematically to exploit it is a tribute to his powers of self-examination and self-integration, to his genius as a methodical adventurer.

The persona of Orion, the mask the poet dons for *Aromates chasseurs*, suits Char's vision as ideally as does the image of the archipelago. The former, moreover, probably grew out of the latter. Orion, it will be recalled, ended as an archipelago in the sky, a constellation. The earliest myth of such a transforma-

tion, Orion no doubt also appeals to Char as a cluster of con-
tradictions, as the hunter hunted, the blinded one who re-
covers his sight (paradoxically, by facing the dazzling rays of
the rising sun), the beloved betrayed (by Artemis). In *Aromates
chasseurs*, Orion has made the return trip to earth, he has come
down from his archipelago in the heavens to live once again
among men, to unite outer space, the power of abstraction and
the laws of science with imagination, feeling and sensuous,
spice-filled existence, to join the cosmos to the concrete. His
task, set forth in the text that serves as a foreword to Char's
collection, is to find the third path, the road that will lead us
out of the prison of false dichotomies:

> *Ce siècle a décidé de l'existence de nos deux espaces immémoriaux: le
> premier, l'espace intime où jouaient notre imagination et nos senti-
> ments; le second, l'espace circulaire, celui du monde concret. Les
> deux étaient inséparables. Subvertir l'un, c'était bouleverser
> l'autre. Les premiers effets de cette violence peuvent être surpris nette-
> ment. Mais quelles sont les lois qui corrigent et redressent ce que les
> lois qui infestent et ruinent ont laissé inachevé? Et sont-ce des lois?
> Y a-t-il des dérogations? Comment s'opère le signal? Est-il un
> troisième espace en chemin, hors du trajet des deux connus? Révolu-
> tion d'Orion resurgi parmi nous.* [45]

If at this point we examine the rest of "Commune prés-
ence," the part that precedes and builds up to the closing
lines, that poem as a whole appears a perfect distillation of
Char's idiosyncratic, contradictory vision:

> Tu es pressé d'écrire
> Comme si tu étais en retard sur la vie
> S'il en est ainsi fais cortège à tes sources
> Hâte-toi
> Hâte-toi de transmettre
> Ta part de merveilleux de rébellion de bienfaisance
> Effectivement tu es en retard sur la vie

La vie inexprimable
La seule en fin de compte à laquelle tu acceptes de t'unir
Celle qui t'est refusée chaque jour par les êtres et par les
    choses
Dont tu obtiens péniblement deci delà quelques fragments
    décharnés
Au bout de combats sans merci
Hors d'elle tout n'est qu'agonie soumise fin grossière
Si tu rencontres la mort durant ton labeur
Reçois-la comme la nuque en sueur trouve bon le mouchoir
    aride
En t'inclinant
Si tu veux rire
Offre ta soumission
Jamais tes armes

Both an art of poetry and an art of living, "Commune pré-
sence" starts out, typically, at full throttle. The first several
lines dramatize what the poet declares elsewhere, that in
living-writing authentically "Nous sommes irrésistiblement
jetés en avant."[46] But even while hurrying forward we must
also link up with our origins ("fais cortège à tes sources"). In
still another paradox we note that the effort to overtake life,
surely more a gesture of taking than of giving, frames the lines
"Hâte-toi/Hâte-toi de transmettre/Ta part de merveilleux de
rébellion de bienfaisance," which affirm giving and not taking.
Furthermore, as Char makes clear, the only life worth living-
writing is the one that remains forever out of reach, forever
"inexprimable." We seek to embrace its wholeness but after
terrible struggles we seize only odd bits and pieces of it.
Somehow or other, too, we must both rebel and submit, resist
and accept. We must hold our heads high and yet bow. Above
all, we must cease to oppose life and death and instead see
them for what they are, aspects of each other.

In "Commune présence" and in one way or another

throughout all of Char, poetry and life are not distinct but coextensive, the former being simply the tragic, contradictory sense of the latter. If in this poem Char expresses both disgust with the idea of submission ("Hors d'elle tout n'est qu'agonie soumise fin grossière") and commitment to it ("Offre ta soumission"), he does so because the two responses co-exist in him. Such contradictions abound in his work, giving it a steady pulse beat and an immense tensile strength, just as they abound in life, causing it to breathe and making it impregnable to any sure penetration, impossible of any definitive sorting out. His poetry creates not symbols which distance us from life but contradictions which draw us ever closer to life's mysterious core, to that leap, that contact and that spark which, paradox of paradoxes, form the vital center of cosmic disintegration:

> Dans le chaos d'une avalanche, deux pierres s'épousant au bond purent s'aimer nues dans l'espace. L'eau de neige qui les engloutit s'étonna de leur mousse ardente.[47]

IV. André du Bouchet

André du Bouchet, one of the most compelling French poets to emerge during the 1945-1960 period, helped to launch the review *L'Ephémère* in 1967. He and Jacques Dupin, both members of the review's editorial board, were also among its most frequent contributors. Their very active participation in the life of the review during the five years of its existence (1967-1972), coupled with their writings on Alberto Giacometti,[1] the virtual patron saint of *L'Ephémère*, suggests that whatever identity *L'Ephémère* possessed was largely one that Du Bouchet and Dupin imparted to it. In their many contributions to the review, they managed to endow it with a certain tone, a tone verging on a theme—that of a persistent and yet continually eroded man-centeredness and of a quest for an absolute that lies forever beyond our grasp. However, in spite of some basic resemblances between them, including an apparently similar conception of art, a common commitment to *L'Ephémère* and a shared reverence for Giacometti, as poets Du Bouchet and Dupin were and remain quite different from each other. Accordingly, I shall consider them separately, treating Du Bouchet in this chapter and Dupin in the next. In both cases I shall examine not only an *oeuvre* but also possible affinities between that *oeuvre* and *L'Ephémère*'s patron saint.

Of the six poets treated in this book, Du Bouchet alone spent a major part of his youth living and studying abroad. Born in 1924 in Paris and raised there until World War II, between the ages of 17 and 24 he was a student in the United States, first at Amherst College and later at Harvard University, where he took an M.A. degree in comparative literature. (He returned to France in 1948 and has lived there ever since.) One direct consequence of his stay in America was an awakening to other literatures—English and German in particular—which, among other things, resulted in his undertaking translations of Shakespeare, Joyce, Hölderlin and Paul Celan.

Critical reactions to two of his translations, sections of Joyce's *Finnegans Wake* and Celan's *Strette*, when juxtaposed with certain observations Du Bouchet has made regarding the role of language and writing in poetry, reveal the gulf that separates *L'Ephémère* from *Tel Quel*, France's latter-day Orphic poets from its contemporary hermeticists. Stephen Heath, in the special "Joyce" number of *Tel Quel*, objects to Du Bouchet's translation of *Finnegans Wake* for its "manques de conscience intertextuelle."[2] Henri Meschonnic, in his review of Du Bouchet's translations of Celan, argues at length for the proposition that "chez Du Bouchet, traduire un poème est en retrait sur écrire."[3] At issue in both of these criticisms is Du Bouchet's essentially non-materialist attitude toward language and writing, an attitude that the poet himself has on at least one occasion formulated quite explicitly:

> For my part, language is not at all the object of my work. I do not work at all on the level of language, or a structure of language. . . . To the degree that in writing, man goes beyond what he is, one operates on the level of language, but one does not stop with language: language is not an end in itself. It remains open, consequently, it remains open on something that is other than language. If there is examination of language, it is not as a closed structure.[4]

As we shall see, Du Bouchet's poetry does indeed remain "open on something that is other than language."

Du Bouchet started publishing poetry in 1946, apparently around the time that he discovered Pierre Reverdy, an event which, by Du Bouchet's own word, had a great impact on him.[5] Not surprisingly, therefore, certain points in common link the two poets, a phenomenon that critics, most notably Jean-Pierre Richard, have not failed to detect. Richard observes, for example, that "comme Reverdy . . . Du Bouchet sera hanté par la notion d'*obstacle*."[6] In addition, we find in both poets a stripped-down, monochrome vocabulary, as well as a shifting left margin, together with sporadic two- or three-word lines (all of which suggests "a spacing of the reading" modeled to some degree after Mallarmé). Another important similarity has been suggested indirectly by Du Bouchet himself in an essay on Reverdy: "La forme immense et vague de l'univers est convoyée par des lignes dures et précises ouvertes de tous les côtés sur le vide: le blanc, l'air, le silence, les pénètre de toutes parts en doigts de gant; textes sapés, rongés, bousculés par le tumulte qui les disperse."[7] This brief, highly evocative description of Reverdy's poetic universe, while accurate as far as it goes, understandably falls somewhat short of saying everything about him that must be said even in a concise, general statement. On the other hand, Du Bouchet focuses here on just those aspects of Reverdy's work that have their counterparts in his own *oeuvre*. Accordingly, one can profitably turn the quote back on Du Bouchet himself, where the shapeless immensity of the universe informs and yet threatens slight, airy but somehow rock-like texts. Du Bouchet's poems, in fact, have a perceptibly harder, less nuanced and more peremptory quality about them than Reverdy's, and possess a stark, elemental lyricism that seems peculiar to Du Bouchet alone. The titles of his two major collections to date, *Dans la chaleur vacante* (Mercure de France, 1961) and *Où le soleil* (Mercure de France, 1968), suggest the ambience of his entire poetic universe, that of a denuded expanse in which solar energy (principally fire, whiteness, heat, light, dryness, and wind) reduces man's presence to near absence, to scattered farm implements and eternally advancing but insubstantial figures.

Jean-Pierre Richard has convincingly shown Du Bouchet's poetry to be a tissue of antinomies, all of which in one way or another involve the dialectic of an autonomous consciousness functioning apart from the world and a dependent consciousness forever "out there" in the world. The perceiving self in Du Bouchet is neither pure subjectivity nor is it dispersed among its perceptions, but rather shuttles endlessly back and forth between these two poles. This to-and-fro motion in Du Bouchet, moreover, is in reality movement forward, it is a quest or, in Richard's words, a "chasse à l'être."[8] I should like to develop Richard's fundamental insight further, principally by examining several poems by Du Bouchet *qua* poems, as coherent wholes, possibly the only thing that Richard does not do in his seminal study. I shall consider first a text from *Dans la chaleur vacante* and then two very brief texts from *Où le soleil*.

"Fraction," from *Dans la chaleur vacante*, typifies Du Bouchet's poetry in a number of ways:

Le lointain est moins distant que le sol, le lit
mordant de l'air,
            où tu t'arrêtes, comme une
herse, sur la terre rougeoyante.

Je reste au-dessus de l'herbe, dans l'air aveuglant.

Le sol fait sans cesse irruption vers nous,
            sans que je m'éloigne
    du jour. (p. 43)

As regards visual-graphic form, the poem consists of three sentences, each of which is set off from the rest by blocks above and below, and two of which, the first and the third, include abbreviated and variously indented lines. The text has, therefore, the somewhat fragmented appearance that we have grown more or less used to encountering in French poetry since Mallarmé and Reverdy. But Du Bouchet differs from his predecessors in the way he exploits the white space of the page to isolate from the whole each part of his poem. This fracturing use of interlinear white space is not found in Reverdy, and while it does occur in "Un coup de dés," it is combined there with the rightward movement of most of the double pages of that text, whereas in Du Bouchet, despite occasional margin shifts, a traditional leftside justification is essentially adhered to, as it is in Reverdy.

Yet other, almost equally obvious features in "Fraction" emphasize cohesion rather than centrifugal drift or separation into parts. For example, the first sentence scans as 12/4/6/8, while the second and third together read as 12/10/6/2. In both "halves" of the poem thus created, the total number of syllables is the same, and the rhythm follows a rubato-like pattern of theme and variation. Also, "tu" in the poem's first sentence and "je'" in the second are collected, so to speak, in the third sentence in "nous" and then fused definitively in the final clause in "je." Thus, rhythmically the poem is balanced, almost symmetrical, while personal pronouns link its first and second sentences individually to the third. Both of these devices, especially as they overlap with each other, tend to unify the poem.

Other formal or, more precisely, stylistic features in "Fraction" further reinforce its unity and cohesiveness. To discuss these I shall have to broach the subject of the poem's thematics. I have already pointed out that the dialectic of consciousness as a kind of independent cogito on the one hand and on the other as scattered, even lost among its perceptions, structures most of Du Bouchet's poetry. "Fraction" is no exception to this general rule. The poem's central contrary notions in this regard are "far-awayness" and "near-at-handness," with the perceiving self, through the personal pronouns, gravitating, quite literally, toward both notions. Lexically this apparent contradiction is rendered in all three sentences in monosyllabic, elemental and paradoxical language. In the first sentence, earth, *le sol*, opposes *l'air*, but is also juxtaposed with it, stretched under it as its "biting bed," its "lit mordant." In the second sentence *l'herbe* and *l'air aveuglant* enact the very same opposition/juxtaposition, while in the third sentence, *sol* and *jour* perform this function. In each sentence, the first term of the opposed/juxtaposed pair suggests here-near and the second, there-far. Furthermore, the repetition in the second sentence of *air*, the second term of the pair presented in sentence one, and the repetition in the third sentence of *sol*, the first term of this pair, constitute the basic textual armature of the poem's inner coherence and wholeness.

Air is without doubt the key word in "Fraction." It signifies both the ether,[9] hence that which is remote and impalpable, i.e., *lointain* (having progressed from *air* through *air aveuglant* to *jour* which, associated as it is with *éloigne*, closes the poem with a muffled echo of the opening *lointain*), and that which is proximate as a palpable, even intruding, presence. This latter quality of *air* becomes obvious when we read the phrase "le lit/mordant de l'air" no longer as appositive with and hence attributive to "le sol" but, for the moment at least, independently of "le sol." The pause between lines one and two, moreover, encourages us to link "mordant," however fleetingly, as much with *air* as with *sol* or *lit*. Also, in the poem's middle sentence we see the final phrase, "l'air aveuglant," functioning both as an intermediary stage between *air* of sentence one and *jour* of sentence three, and as an unambiguous assertion of *air*'s thick intrusiveness, its capacity not only to light with its brightness (the aspect of *air aveuglant* that anticipates *jour*), but also to blind, to possess as impinging quasi-solidity—a capacity that reinforces, and is in turn reinforced by *air*'s momentary but telling alliance with "mordant" in the first sentence. *Air* is thus the most richly ambiguous word in the poem, since it expresses, in the terminology I proposed earlier, both here-near and there-far. The specific nature of *air*'s ambiguity identifies it as the medium through which the dialectic between here and there, near and far, operates in "Fraction."

This brings us back to the theme in "Fraction" of consciousness as reciprocal action between here-near and there-far. Elsewhere in *Dans la chaleur vacante* we read:

> . . . Je ne sais pas si je suis ici
> ou là,
>   Dans l'air ou dans l'ornière. Ce sont des
> morceaux d'air que je foule comme des mottes. . . . (p. 59)

Consciousness for Du Bouchet thus tramps forward, paradoxically, on clods of air. It is bounded by its path or bed, thus is an entity unto itself, and yet it is forever flowing to and existing at the farthest point of its perceptions, where it is dispersed (or "perdue," in Du Bouchet's lexicon) rather than contained (or "liée," as Du Bouchet would have it). In "Fraction," as we have seen, the perceiving self is likened to a harrow slicing through clods of earth toward a *lointain* that is as far away as the *jour* and yet as close at hand as the biting, blinding *air*. The breaking prow of the harrow (hence the poem's title?) symbolizes consciousness dug in and working a single earth, underfoot *and* in the distance, at one with its own immediate tracing-open action, its scoring, *and* with the unfolding edge of perceptual experience cresting on the horizon.

This reciprocal and dialectical conception of consciousness is very close to phenomenology's notion of intentionality, which also views consciousness as a pre-reflexive condition in which the perceiving self is imbedded dynamically in the world around it. But more than Husserl (or Char) "Fraction" recalls Mallarmé, for whom "on n'écrit, lumineusement, sur champ obscur, l'alphabet des astres, seul, ainsi s'indique, ébauché ou interrompu; l'homme poursuit noir sur blanc." Immediately before the lines just quoted, we find the inkwell characterized as "cristal comme une conscience." Consciousness for Mallarmé is thus transparent, empty except for "sa goutte, au fond, de ténèbres," the capacity to go out of itself in a dark tracing across a white expanse. Earlier on in the same text the poet asserts that "méditer sans traces devient évanescent," from which we may infer the corollary that for Mallarmé to meditate *with* traces, to write, would be to stylize forever the fleeting activity of consciousness.[10] Du Bouchet's harrow-consciousness would seem to cut across a denuded expanse in the same way that Mallarmé's man pursues black on white. Both moving figures suggest a stylus scoring a blank page, re-cording for all time the evanescent drama of consciousness.

Où le soleil confirms and clarifies much of what we have seen in *Dans la chaleur vacante*, particularly in "Fraction." At the same time, Du Bouchet's second major collection has a more concentrated impact on the reader than did his first. We notice immediately, for example, that *Où le soleil* has no pagination and that on virtually any given page large areas of white space surround the print, thereby isolating the lines and line clusters even more completely than was the case in *Dans la chaleur va-cante*. Almost as quickly we sense a functional relationship or interdependence between the absence of pagination and the generous use of white space on the one hand, and on the other, the texts themselves. We sense that the obtrusive whiteness of pages uncluttered by numbers somehow mimes the denuded expanse across which the word tracings of consciousness stead-ily advance.

Another source of the sharply focused impact of *Où le soleil* is the now starker, more simplified, and more integrated nature of Du Bouchet's poetic universe. It is a universe in which every important element is semantically contiguous to at least one other key element, in which meaning is founded upon contras-tive pairs of words, images or notions, and in which the drama of consciousness is all. All three aspects of *Où le soleil*, moreover, are so thoroughly fused that it is difficult at first to separate them from one another. On closer inspection, how-ever, the volume reveals itself as a continuum in which high frequency words such as *paille* and *meule* connect in a seamless web not only with each other but also in series with terms such as *faux, été, soleil, feu* and so forth. Also, a seemingly endless number of antinomies form the very warp and woof of this fabric. Such pairs usually follow the opposition/juxtaposition pattern or structure that we found in "Fraction." Often they involve or reduce to hot/cold, here/there, intimately human/ cosmically inanimate, repetition/single occurrence, and earth/ sun. All tie back in one way or another to the motif of consciousness as residing in both its own agency or functioning and in the result of that functioning: "si nous sommes ce qui a crié/et le cri" (from "Ajournement").

Yves Bonnefoy has referred to André du Bouchet as "ce moins cartésien des poètes."[11] In so doing Bonnefoy was perhaps thinking of the radical rejection of the subject-object dichotomy which Du Bouchet's poetry implies. Be that as it may, at least one very slight text in *Où le soleil*, entitled "Etage," enacts such a radical rejection:

> Demain, au-dessous de la terre, encore (j'ai
> sombré, couru) le coutre, comme tu t'incorpores
> au jour,
>   s'accoude
>   au vent.

Once again a cutting farm implement, this time *le coutre*, the frontmost disc or blade of a plowshare, is assimilated to a questing human faculty, to consciousness, through its association with *je* and *tu*. Once again earth and air are interchangeable ("comme tu t'incorpores au jour"). Now, however, over/ under is as important a contrastive pair as here/there. The over/under pair or layering image, suggested already in the poem's title and picked up in the text in *au-dessous, sombré, s'accoude* and even *coutre*, in fact pervades *Où le soleil*. Depending on context, this image expresses the search for transcendence, for something beyond the given, beyond experience (as in a poem entitled "Oublié, ici . . .") *or* the acceptance of the impossibility of just such a penetration of the here and now (as in "Cette surface"). Whether immanent or transcendent, however, the movement of consciousness, like a tropism, in a sense simply happens to us; logically it is first cosmic, elemental, and then personal, intimate (as "Station" shows).

"Araire," another very brief text in *Où le soleil*, gives us a slightly different perspective on the drama of consciousness:

> La jante du froid, que
> l'air en avant de nous, façonne—et sans retour, comme
> l'éclat.
> Elle.

Again the frontmost part of a plow slices through the earth. This time, however, the cutting farm implement is mentioned only in the title. In the text it becomes the wheel rim of the cold formed by the onrushing air at our front, and thus concretely symbolizes the leading edge of our ever probing consciousness. The poem abruptly narrows toward both the plow-consciousness as picket or point and the single-occurrence, non-repetitive, pioneering nature of this implement in action. Closing his text with an isolated *Elle*, Du Bouchet endows the implement with a mode of being that eradicates distinctions between itself and what it functions in or against, hence between subject and object. For the plow of consciousness is seen as inhering not really in itself—*araire*, significantly, is a masculine noun and thus not directly evoked by *Elle*—but in the reciprocal action that it accomplishes jointly with all that is in front of it.

As Jean-Pierre Richard intimated more than a decade ago and as my discussion thus far would, I trust, tend to bear out, the premise that consciousness is a pre-reflexive, unitary condition—with all the yearning for a lost paradise that such a premise can imply—undergirds Du Bouchet's entire *oeuvre*. From this we might infer that here is a poet whose basic intention is to build access routes, for himself and his reader, to such primal states as innocence and immediacy. And yet everything else about his work from its dispersed visual-graphic form to the dwarfed, fragmented status of the human figures in it, neutralizes whatever feeling of presence or plenitude it might otherwise evoke. Clearly in Du Bouchet there is a felt need for an absolute such as being, contact with which would doubtless satisfy the deepest longings of both poet and reader. This very contact, moreover, would appear to be the principal *raison d'être* of the quest motif that virtually structures his work. But Du Bouchet's quest is endless precisely because no sustained contact with being seems possible.

The literal shape of being is glimpsed, sporadically and in peripheral vision as it were, throughout Du Bouchet. For him (as for many others before him) it takes the form of the universe revealed as a macrocosm of man. In *Dans la chaleur vacante*, and even more so in *Où le soleil*, the dark stylus-figure advancing across the white page-expanse encounters bits and pieces of itself writ large. Thus the wind is referred to most often by the word *souffle* rather than by *vent*. Parts of the body, such as *le front* or *le genou*, are come upon "out there." However, recognition is never complete, the *paysage* never quite becomes a *visage*. Is the Great Figure, then, in reality discovered outside, or is it merely a wishful projection from within? Du Bouchet gives no definitive answer to this fundamental question, but he poses it, and expresses the hunger for an answer to it, in unforgettable fashion.

Since *Où le soleil* appeared in 1968, Du Bouchet has published more *poésie critique* than poetry, even if the line between the two genres has in his case grown increasingly blurred over the years. New poems by him under the titles "Laisses" and "Poèmes," appeared in *L'Ephémère*, Nos. 19-20 (hiver-printemps 1972), pp. 320-28, and *Argile*, No. 8 (automne 1975), pp. 5-13. For sheer verbal substance, however, these spare texts can hardly match the dense pages that make up ". . . sur un coin éclaté," the essay in *poésie critique* that Du Bouchet also published in *L'Ephémère*, Nos. 19-20 (pp. 428-49). Inspired by and interspersed with ink drawings by Louis Bruzon, ". . . sur un coin éclaté" weaves an elaborate web of images on the theme of verticality, which the poet obviously sees as central to Bruzon's drawings, almost as if he aspired to create the homologue in words of the artist's *encres*. As for the books published during this same period, in 1972 Du Bouchet brought out *Qui n'est pas tourné vers nous* (Mercure de France), a volume comprising six long pieces on Giacometti followed by a one-page poem entitled "Air"; and in 1975 he published *La Couleur* (Le Collet de Buffle), a twenty-six-page, unpaginated, large-format *plaquette* in response to the work of Bram van Velde.

Du Bouchet's devoting an entire book to Giacometti in 1972 comes as no surprise to anyone familiar with the poet's earlier writings and career. In 1968 he had published *Alberto Giacometti, 1901-1966* (Galerie Claude Bernard). Also, no fewer than four of the six essays in *Qui n'est pas tourné vers nous* had appeared earlier in *L'Ephémère*.[12] Furthermore, as a founding editor of *L'Ephémère* and as the review's most frequent contributor, Du Bouchet was presumably involved in the decision to make the review's inaugural issue essentially a homage to Giacometti and to carry a Giacometti nude on the cover of all twenty of its numbers.

But even as early as 1961 in *Dans la chaleur vacante* one can sense a profound kinship between the poet and Giacometti. Problems involving space or, more precisely, the perception of space (e.g., remoteness, proximity, to-and-fro movement between them) haunt both poet and artist, as does the notion of a universe steadily though never completely stripping itself of the human. Like Giacometti, Du Bouchet is obsessed by a problematically visible, stick-thin (or stylus-sized) advancing figure. Also, poet and artist keep man, though radically diminished, at the very center of their universe, and in both the search for an absolute remains the unwavering purpose of creative activity. Finally, each man confronts the problem of space directly and attempts to solve it with arbitrary means and in diametrically opposite ways, the sculptor by establishing for every one of his pieces a specific, finite viewing distance, and the poet (in *Où le soleil*) by incorporating infinite space into his page through the device of scattering his lines, line fragments and line clusters across unpaginated and hence limitless white expanses.

In contrast to *Dans la chaleur vacante* and *Où le soleil, Qui n'est pas tourné vers nous* represents a conscious, extended development on Du Bouchet's part of what Giacometti's work means to him. Certain themes relating to air (and thus to the book's closing text, "Air," as well as to key images in earlier poems like "Fraction")—heat, whiteness, silence, space, nothingness—gradually converge across the six essays, giving the book a subtle cumulative power. Paralleling this convergence is the recurring paradoxical notion that as an artist Giacometti makes by unmaking, that while adding to what is he moves always toward what is not, toward emptiness. This and comparable paradoxes, antinomies and contradictions fill these pages, suggesting that the poet is fascinated by the artist's work because it brings him to a level of reflection quite above his usual response to "art." Significantly, Du Bouchet entitled one of his essays "Tournant au plus vite le dos au fatras de l'art."

One idea seems to pervade the book, though not in obvious fashion. Two of the essay titles broach this idea more directly than does any single utterance in the various texts: "Plus loin que le regard une figure" and (the book's title piece) "Qui n'est pas tourné vers nous." For Du Bouchet, Giacometti's works remain immutably ˜remote, strangely out of range of our glance, independent of our looking at them and indifferent to us. Yet we of course see them and in so doing realize that the uncrossable chasm, the distance, *l'air*, that separates us from them also joins us to them. Our experience of Giacometti's art thus brings us face to face with the essential contradiction, the inherently dyadic nature of consciousness itself. But consciousness functions within an overarching structure that is unitary: "Mais le sol même est figure" (p. 126); "Etre—et non . . . même tenant" (p. 156). Giacometti's entropizing figures, "poussières sculptées" (p. 135), "dansant . . . disparaissant" (p. 136), ultimately ground us, if only fleetingly, in that which encompasses consciousness.

Qui n'est pas tourné vers nous is an absorbing if in some ways frustrating book. Between the first essay and the sixth, Du Bouchet's style grows increasingly notational and private. Weighted in favor of criticism at the start, by the end of the volume poetry clearly predominates. In this sense Du Bouchet offers us a fair sampling of the possibilities of *poésie critique*, a kind of introduction to the genre, as well as to its limitations. While he succeeds in deepening our appreciation of Giacometti, he at the same time whets but does not satisfy our appetite for something else, for texts that are free of a fixed referent, for poetry itself.

The fixed referent in the case of *La Couleur*, as I have already noted, is Bram van Velde. With this brief, unpaginated work, the line between essay and poem seems even less distinct, the tone more personal and the language closer to sense experience, especially visual, than was the case in *Qui n'est pas tourné vers nous*. Where the essays on Giacometti tended to avoid the first person singular and to gravitate toward the abstract, *La Couleur*, replete with "je," re-enacts the poet's unmediated encounter with "peintures de Bram van Velde réunies en grand nombre." Du Bouchet, now freed of his bodily weight, rises out of himself through his eyes to the realm of pure color, borne aloft by an "emportement qui déborde, laisse transparaître, pareil à la couleur pure, le moment dont on ne se rapproche pas." Like Reverdy and Char and unlike Ponge, Du Bouchet thus views art as a way of acceding to a translinguistic, ineffable reality. Also, thanks to Van Velde, color and warmth, outer and inner, fuse for him: "Cela n'est pas l'espace, mais une parcelle de la brutalité des dehors—que je retrouve en moi chaleur, couleur, quand je me recompose." Subject and object, warmth and color, moreover, dissolve in perfect reciprocity, "l'épanchement de la couleur allant ses chemins, moi-même cheminant du mien." Thus Du Bouchet's most recent *poésie critique*, in harmony with *Qui n'est pas tourné vers nous* and with his poetry early and late, dramatizes a relentlessly post-Cartesian, anti-Romantic consciousness.

The fact that throughout his *oeuvre* and regardless of genre Du Bouchet renders the dyadic structure of consciousness and that he situates consciousness within the framework of a quest, suggests that he is drawn to epistemological and ontological concerns rather than to standard poetic themes. But the very refusal to stick to traditional themes for the lyric (i.e., love, death, time's flight, the seasons, etc.) typifies all four poets whose work I have examined up to this point. A thoroughgoing methodical adventurer, Du Bouchet, like Reverdy, Ponge and Char before him, combines poetry and philosophy naturally. Also, "burning Reason," rhapsodic reflection," defines his *poésie critique* at least as much as it does Apollinaire's. If in contrast to Ponge (and Valéry), poetic composition, either in general or within a particular text folding back on itself, is rarely if ever a suitable "subject" for Du Bouchet, *Qui n'est pas tourné vers nous* and *La Couleur* subvert genre distinctions between analytical and imaginative writing as effectively as "Le Soleil placé en abîme" and "Le Pré" do. Finally, after Reverdy and Char, Du Bouchet sees man in an essentially cosmic perspective and grapples ultimately with metaphysical questions to the exclusion of all else.

A poet's esthetic stance and vision of life often are traced as accurately in the constellation of his heroes as in the substance of his writings. As we have seen, Du Bouchet, no exception to this rule, especially admires Reverdy, Giacometti and Bram van Velde. To this list we must add the name of Hölderlin, an anthology of whose poems, selected and translated into French

by Du Bouchet, appeared in 1963.[13] Hölderlin, it will be re-
called, is the premier modern figure in Heidegger's pantheon,
occupying in the German philosopher's intellectual scheme of
things a position of importance comparable to that of the pre-
Socratics. In the context of the present study the mere mention
of Heidegger and the pre-Socratic thinkers calls to mind René
Char, Heidegger's favorite French poet and another great ad-
mirer of Heraclitus. Significantly, the creative artists just
named—Reverdy, Giacometti, Bram van Velde, Hölderlin,
Char and Du Bouchet himself—share at least one basic value:
for all of them art, whether painting, sculpture or poetry, is
simply a means, albeit an indispensable and quasi-sacred one,
and not an end in itself. It is the royal road to that place that
lies on the other side of art where the cosmic and the human
intersect. What Samuel Beckett, the undisputed master of the
entropic vision, has observed regarding Bram and Geer van
Velde applies with equal pertinence, *mutatis mutandis*, to Re-
verdy, Char and Du Bouchet: "C'est qu'au fond la peinture ne
les intéresse pas. Ce qui les intéresse, c'est la condition
humaine."[14]

V. Jacques Dupin

Jacques Dupin and André du Bouchet are an instructive study in similarities and contrasts. In several important respects Dupin's career as a writer parallels that of Du Bouchet. Both poets made their début in the world of letters between 1945 and 1950. For both, the Surrealist current in French poetry provided the essential matrix. For both, Giacometti has been, and doubtless still is, the artist most to be revered, just as throughout the five years of its life (1967-1972) *L'Ephémère* was the poetry review most deserving of their support. Yet in other, equally important ways these poets differ, not least in their response to *L'Ephémère* as a force in their creative lives. At one stage in his evolution as a poet, for example, Dupin changed directions perceptibly, in part it would seem as a result of his close association with *L'Ephémère*. No comparable shift can be detected in Du Bouchet, in whose case, moreover, any influence between poet and magazine would more probably have worked in the opposite direction.

Unlike Du Bouchet, Dupin was not a founding editor of *L'Ephémère*, but he contributed to the review at regular intervals from No. 2 onward, by No. 7 had joined its editorial board and as of No. 9 held the post of "gérant," roughly the equivalent of managing editor. Since *L'Ephémère* never had an editor (or "directeur"), Dupin in effect eventually ran the review. Presumably this task devolved upon him because he was head of publications for Galerie Maeght, which published *L'Ephémère*. On the other hand, Dupin's personal commitment to the review may also have deen deeper than that of his colleagues. At the very least, his greater material involvement with it from early on is attested by an article on *L'Ephémère* that appeared in early 1968.[1] Bonnefoy, Du Bouchet and Dupin are all mentioned in this article, but Dupin alone is the subject of a biographical sketch, which indicates that even before he assumed the position of "gérant" he was perceived outside the review as *primus inter pares* on its editorial board.

The article in question also includes a brief description of *L'Ephémère*'s view of poetry and purpose as a magazine: "*L'Ephémère* a pour origine le sentiment qu'il existe une approche du réel dont l'oeuvre poétique est seulement le moyen. . . . Le but de *L'Ephémère*, c'est de créer un lieu où ce souci de la vraie fin poétique . . . pourrait se retrouver plus intense" (pp. 16-17). Ironically, while running *L'Ephémère* Dupin would find it increasingly difficult to identify with this near classic formulation of the "Orphic" conception of poetry. He would draw away from Du Bouchet's ontological questing and toward, if never all the way to, the metapoetic stance of Marcelin Pleynet, Directeur-Gérant of *Tel Quel*. It is as if his experience with *L'Ephémère* led Dupin to re-examine his esthetic assumptions and in the process to re-orient himself as a poet.

The review's title and cover design offer a clue to the nature of the change that Dupin underwent during this time. Not long ago George Steiner reminded us that "the dominant trope of Western literate culture calls for the creation of poetic and plastic forms 'that shall outlast bronze and break the tooth of time.' "[2] What are we to make, then, of an elegantly turned-out review of poetry, art criticism and graphics that is called *L'Ephémère*? Are we once again dealing with the type of antiphrasis that Breton and his friends employed when they decided to dub their review *Littérature*? In a sense we are, although the rather heavy sarcasm of Dada days has given way in the intervening half-century to a somewhat subtler brand of irony. For what is incongruous about *L'Ephémère* is not just the gap between what the name suggests and what the review in fact stands for (the case of *Littérature*), but the discrepancy between the review's title on the one hand and its contents and physical attributes on the other. Its sumptuous design and solid material makeup contrast sharply with the flimsy format of the countless ephemeral "little" magazines that are spawned every year on both sides of the Atlantic. Also, the texts and artworks that fill the pages of *L'Ephémère* have precisely that aura of high seriousness which in times past would have guaranteed their at least aspiring to "outlast bronze and break the tooth of time."

Heightened and transposed, the same tension between the evanescent and the permanent, between destructive time and creative eternity, defines the purely graphic dimension of each *L'Ephémère* cover, where the frail specter of a Giacometti nude seems ready to fall away into the neutral background. More vividly and less ambiguously than the review's title, its cover design articulates a Giacometti principle which with time has become increasingly important for Dupin, that the artist must engage destruction itself in his enterprise. According to Dupin, Giacometti makes by stripping away: "Giacometti va du connu à l'inconnu par un dépouillement et une ascèse progressifs. Il s'acharne sur les apparences et creuse le réel jusqu'à rendre visible l'essence de leur rapport, c'est-à-dire la présence d'un sacré."[3] It is precisely this marriage of making, moving forward with breaking, removing, that links Giacometti's art and Dupin's poetry, as these observations, inspired by the latter's collection *L'Embrasure*, reflect: "He [Dupin] writes to destroy continually, yet edification occurs in the very act of demolishing. Each poem is both a destruction and a permanently flawed construction."[4]

For both Dupin and Giacometti, the ultimate destruction of all recognizable form, entropy itself, participates in and indeed permits creation. It should come as no surprise therefore that of the six poets studied in this book, Dupin alone has actually used the word "entropie" in his writing. The term appears in "La Ligne de rupture," a text that was first published in 1970 (in *L'Ephémère*),[5] more than twenty years after the poet's name had begun to appear in print. In an important sense, his entire *oeuvre* can be seen as the inexorable movement toward and then through all that "entropie" implies in the esthetic, moral and metaphysical realms.

Like Du Bouchet, Dupin is an admirer and an astute reader of that older partisan of entropy, Pierre Reverdy. He wrote a moving poetic tribute for the January 1962 *Mercure de France* homage to Reverdy, and in the spring of 1970 was involved in organizing, first at the Fondation Maeght in Saint-Paul-de-Vence and then at the Musée National d'Art Moderne in Paris, "A la rencontre de Pierre Reverdy et ses amis," a highly successful exhibit of paintings, photographs, letters, manuscripts, deluxe editions and other documents centering on the poet's life. In his preface to the catalog for this exhibit, Dupin addresses his own entropic obsessions as much as he does Reverdy's: "De révélation nous n'acceptons que celle qui nous répète, jusqu'à l'incantation, que le monde dérive et se morcelle."[6]

Dupin, however, is more a disciple or at least a protégé of René Char than he is of Reverdy. Born in 1927, twenty years after Char, Dupin received eloquent support from the older poet as early as 1950: "Jacques Dupin ne saurait être ni découvert ni proposé à l'attention des guetteurs de l'imperturbable continent. Tout de suite on a accordé à ses poèmes l'importance que l'on aurait justement refusée aux confidences d'un simple mal d'enfance."[7] In 1971 Dupin returned the compliment with an essay in which he makes some large claims for Char's achievement: "René Char est le seul, à partir de l'illumination rimbaldienne, à avoir approfondi, extrait et mis en oeuvre, poussé à ses limites extrêmes, les immenses possibilités du langage, verticalement exploré."[8] As one might guess from such superlatives, Dupin's enthusiasm for Char at times shades off into emulation. This is particularly true of his early writings, although traces of Char's influence on Dupin can be found throughout his practice. Many a poem by either man, for example, is enormously difficult of access in rather the same way. George Mounin's apt remark in reference to Char ("il y a chez lui plus d'un texte intransmissible, ou qui le restera longtemps")[9] would in fact apply just as appropriately to Dupin. With both men a prose poem especially can have a truly forbidding density. In addition, there are between these poets thematic, lexical and tonal resemblances. Childhood as a persistent state, mountains, torrents, slopes, all bathed in an atmosphere of strength, vigor and resistance—such elements are found in Char and Dupin. Beyond this point, however, the two part company, the older taking the high road to a "tensed serenity" and the younger the low road to something quite different.

Dupin's first major collection of poetry, *Gravir*, which appeared in 1963, contains a number of texts that in one way or another testify to Char's impact on the younger poet. "Ce tison la distance," for example, a series of nine poetic aphorisms, recalls similar sequences by Char, such as "A la santé du serpent," "Rougeur des matinaux," "La Bibliothèque est en feu" and "Les Compagnons dans le jardin." (This last sequence, appropriately enough, is dedicated to Du Bouchet and Dupin.) As did Char's pieces earlier, Dupin's short prose texts blend the lyrical with the didactic, while ranging in tone from concrete truism to Sybilline utterance:

> Dans la connaissance du fleuve la pile de pont l'emporte sur la barque.

> Dévore tes enfants avant qu'ils ne creusent ta fosse, c'est-à-dire sans perdre une nuit.

> Il n'y a qu'une femme qui me suive, et elle ne me suit pas. Pendant que ses habits brûlent, immense est la rosée.[10]

"L'Initiale," also from *Gravir*, echoes another Char:

Poussière fine et sèche dans le vent,
Je t'appelle, je t'appartiens.
Poussière, trait pour trait,
Que ton visage soit le mien,
Inscrutable dans le vent. (p. 59).

Windblown dust called to, sought after, as the poet's own in-
scrutable face reminds us of Char's two-line "Lyre":

Lyre sans bornes des poussières,
Surcroît de notre coeur. [11]

The image of scattering particles in "L'Initiale," moreover, is
central to Char's poetry generally, where, as we have seen,
turned into a rising swarm it acquires positive value. The title
of Dupin's text suggests a similar reversal of normally associ-
ated values. First letters after all bespeak beginnings, coming
into being, not endings, disintegration. And the tone of
"L'Initiale," one of apostrophic, confident entreaty, echoes the
couplet that closes Char's supremely important "Commune
présence": "Essaime la poussière/Nul ne décèlera votre union."

In an important sense, Dupin has come into his own as a
poet only since *Gravir* (1963). Perhaps the best way to trace
the direction in which he has moved since the appearance of his
first major collection of poetry is to examine *L'Embrasure*, his
second such collection, published in 1969. The title of this
collection refers to a window recess, an opening in a wall. As a
literary convention, an *embrasure*, with its *banquette* or window
seat, is a trysting place for lovers, or the ideal spot for a private
conversation. In a military context, an *embrasure* is a crenel in
the wall of a fort, the opening that accommodates a gun barrel.
Finally, the word *embrasure* is only a syllable away from *em-
brasement*, a word that denotes either a totally destructive con-
flagration or the very constructive light of a nocturnal illumi-
nation. The entire semantic and associative halo of *embrasure*

obviously interests Dupin, for the image of an opening or a breach made in that which is normally solid and impenetrable, especially such an image accompanied by the notion of abrupt, even violent and violating passage or communication either through words or within words from one realm to another, dominates his poetry:

> Ouverte en peu de mots,
> comme par un remous, dans quelque mur,
> une embrasure, pas même une fenêtre
>
> pour maintenir à bout de bras
> cette contrée de nuit où le chemin se perd,
>
> à bout de forces une parole nue[12]

As this brief untitled poem shows, the breach or opening in Dupin occurs abruptly, almost convulsively ("comme par un remous"); it is a difficult and even desperate act ("pour maintenir à bout de bras," "à bout de forces . . ."), stark and spare in its simplicity ("Ouverte en peu de mots," ". . . une parole nue"). Whether the breach is made within words or through words ("*en* peu de mots") to something else remains unclear. In this connection, the first line of the poem is just as ambiguous as are its last three lines. The first line, moreover, can easily be construed as linking up with the poem's final three words, and when it does it gives the text a focus and a thrust that are fully in keeping with the poem's central image of the breach. Is language, then, the mere vehicle of transcendence, of penetration to another, deeper reality, or is it the very reality whose depths are to be plumbed? This, for Dupin, is a fundamental question, one which will haunt much of his poetry.

Dupin's obsession with transcendence either through or in language or, more precisely, *l'écriture*, attains its most elaborate expression in *Moraines*, a sequence in *L'Embrasure* of thirty-four untitled prose pieces. This sequence possesses certain formal poetic qualities: specifically it partakes of prose poetry, *poésie critique* and the unique genre to which Francis Ponge's *Proêmes* belongs. It has, to illustrate my point, the peculiarly decisive, even imperious, tone of Char's prose poetry; the lyric, subtly transposed expositions that characterize *poésie critique*; and the explicit concern with language, writing and related matters that mark Ponge's *Proêmes*. Nevertheless, I do not think that *Moraines* qualifies as poetry in the strictest sense of the term, that it comprises texts in which signifier and signified coincide. In the discussion that follows, it is the narrow but deep space that lies between signifier and signified in *Moraines*, the space of meaning, that I should like to explore.

As a title, *Moraines* in a sense prepares us for a post-apocalyptic setting, thereby shaping to some extent our very perception of the texts that go to make up the sequence. Thus, in the perspective of the title, *Moraines* comprises so many heaps of verbal debris left in the wake of a flood or a glacier. On the other hand, the texts themselves, though hardly contradicting the apocalyptic mood conjured up by the title, tend to situate the final debacle temporally either in progress or in prospect and not so much as having already occurred. But whether past, present or future, what precisely is it that for Dupin constitutes the great leveler, the definitive destroyer? On one occasion he seems to identify it with the bulldozer-like advance of technological progress (p. 85). On another he appears to associate it with the ineluctable reification of modern man, including himself (p. 71). What is also clear, however, is that for Dupin something arising out of man's need to create may survive the disaster, particularly if that something created is verbal (p. 84).

Dupin's attitude toward the apocalypse is ambivalent. Darkness, with all that it connotes of final formlessness, for example, is by no means an unequivocally negative value in *Moraines*. The distressful burden of life's essential darkness is to be embraced and the terminal fall of all and everything even hastened. Only thus can we hope to pass through the night to its *retournement*, where it shows its other face, that of light and form, of being as opposed to non-being. Words joined together, while admittedly unreliable, are the force which "laisse surgir le corps ruisselant et le visage éclairé d'une réalité tout autre que celle qu'on avait poursuivie et piégée dans la nuit" (p. 95). Thus, thanks to a verbal ordering, another reality, albeit an unexpected one, surfaces. Here as elsewhere in *Moraines* a breakthrough from one realm to another occurs, thanks to "l'illumination fixe de quelque mots inespérément accordés" (p. 64). Language keeps its last secrets from the poet, for it has powers which are beyond his ken and beside which he is as nothing (p. 91). Still, the poet knows that he must "donner à voir" precisely that which he cannot see and which, inadvertently as it were, "le langage en se déployant heurte et découvre" (p. 69). He knows too that the rise of being entails a breaking open, a breach, and that what comes into being will do so still streaming with non-being ("le corps ruisselant").

Non-being in *Moraines*, that which must be breached, is rendered by a cluster of semantically related terms: *mur* (or *muraille*), *nuit, mer, terre, forêt*, and *opacité*, all of which suggest varying degrees of impenetrability. The quest for being, as we have seen, is usually associated in *Moraines* with the image of breaking open, and this image, in turn, often involves the lining up of words, that is, writing. One text in the sequence is particularly instructive, not only as regards the close relationship that Dupin sees existing between writing and breaking open, but also as regards the element of violation and destruction that for Dupin must attend the creative act:

Commencer comme on déchire un drap, le drap dans les plis duquel on se regardait dormir. L'acte d'écrire comme rupture, et engagement cruel de l'esprit, et du corps, dans une succession nécessaire de ruptures, de dérives, d'embrasements. Jeter sa mise entière sur le tapis, toutes ses armes et son souffle, et considérer ce don de soi comme un déplacement imperceptible et presque indifférent de l'équilibre universel. Rompre et ressaisir, et ainsi renouer. Dans la forêt nous sommes plus près du bûcheron que du promeneur solitaire. Pas de contemplation innocente. Plus de hautes futaies traversées de rayons et de chants d'oiseaux, mais des stères de bois en puissance. Tout nous est donné, mais pour être forcé, pour être entamé, en quelque façon pour être détruit,—et nous détruire. (p. 76)

In the forest of non-being the poet is closer, significantly, to the woodsman than he is to the solitary walker, for his task is to cut, to "savage" into being "stères de bois en puissance." In potency, because, as we have seen, creation is blind, it is an act whose consequences remain forever hidden from the agent.

The theme of *l'écriture* as the vehicle of transcendence, as the means of making visible that which is both ephemeral and beyond writing, the theme of building as breaking, of writing as violating, and the theme of poetic creation as the act of doing something whose meaning exceeds the poet's personal, conscious vision even as it justifies his repetitive and seemingly trivial activity—these three central themes in *Moraines* come together in one text:

Migrations incessantes des mots jusqu'au dernier à travers l'écriture, tentative pour rendre un seul instant visible à leur crête celui qui disparaît déjà. Le sentiment de la perfectibilité de leur marche et de la fragilité de leur liaison tend à me persuader de mon pouvoir d'en finir. A me persuader qu'à la fin quelque chose d'édifié et de rompu à la fois affrontera la mort avec des yeux qui ne sont pas les miens. Et manifestera le caractère fortuit, accidental, insignifiant de ma disparition. Comme l'allégresse d'un rayon de soleil brisé sur la paroi tout à coup privé d'ombre et de sens.

De cet édifice hors de vue, et inimaginable, j'élimine les
matériaux incompatibles avec sa nature, avec son dessein.
Incapable d'en esquisser les lignes ou d'en supputer la
hauteur, j'arpente le sol de sa base, j'attends de l'écriture
seule qu'elle en indique l'orientation et le tracé, je pèse et
j'interroge de la main les pierres avancées, je saisis et je re-
jette avec l'obscur instinct de la bête avertie des nourritures
qui lui sont néfastes. Et je jalonne l'étroitesse de mon ter-
ritoire, je sonde l'aridité de son sous-sol.

Ficher en terre ferme un pieu, un second pieu, à l'infini le
même pieu, sans que se dresse la moindre palissade,—à quoi
se réduit et par quoi recommence toute entreprise d'édifier.
(p. 74)

But there is ambiguity here in Dupin's conception of the role
of writing. Facing toward "cet édifice hors de vue, et inima-
ginable," he states, we note, "j'attends de l'écriture seule
qu'elle en indique l'orientation et le tracé, je pèse et j'inter-
roge de la main les pierres avancées, je saisis et je rejette avec
l'obscur instinct de la bête avertie des nourritures qui lui
sont néfastes." But if the true guides to poetic creation inhere
in the act of writing itself, wherein lies the truth of the fin-
ished poem? Or, indeed, will the finished poem embody any
transcendent truth at all? And can the poet ever really convince
himself that his creation will realize itself, become meaning-
ful, at some future time?

The above text invites such questions, questions that be-
speak a malaise that the poet expresses more directly elsewhere
in *Moraines*, as when, for example, he concedes that "l'écriture
ne nous rend rien" (p. 63); or when he admits, ruefully, that
he cannot keep from imagining being as something separate
from himself even though he knows that he is part of it (p. 67);
or when, in still another text, we come across two rather bleak
inversions within the sequence's apparent value system, state-
ments in which the image of the breach and night as a meta-

phor for non-being lash back at the poet, so to speak (p. 94).
On the other hand we have just witnessed the poet concluding
a key text with this telling claim: "Tout nous est donné, mais
pour être forcé, pour être entamé, en quelque façon pour être
détruit,—et nous détruire." The act of creating, of forming for
Dupin is therefore an all-encompassing gesture of destruction.
It involves de-forming, de-structuring, not only the given but
oneself as well.

Against the background of the central themes in *Moraines*
and of the doubts, uncertainties and risks that accompany
them, the title of this sequence and the title of the volume in
which it appears, *L'Embrasure*, take on a new resonance.
Clearly Dupin sees the poetic act as Promethean in scale and in
intent. Having given up all hope of regaining lost Eden and
profoundly dissatisfied with things as they are, in a grandiose
and perhaps ultimately futile leap, he anticipates the Apoca-
lypse, he absorbs the leveling power of the final catastrophe
into his texts and in so doing just might transcend the end
point of entropy itself. But nothing is certain in this project
save the writing. It either makes or is the breach, *l'embrasure*,
the momentary flash or opening in the dark night of non-
being, beyond which the writing will form *moraines*, eloquent
monuments or silent rubble, who can say? For everything that
concerns the poetic project is problematic—and the problema-
tic may be all there is.

Of the several major texts that Dupin has published since
L'Embrasure (1969), one in particular, "Un Récit,"[13] develops
themes that the poet first explored systematically in *Moraines*.
Most notably, in "Un Récit" as in *Moraines*, catastrophe, in-
cluding self-destruction, is raised to the level of a first
principle of creation:

> les figures du récit ne s'élèvent à la lisibilité qu'à la
> faveur, et dans la lumière, du désastre. Il leur faut nous
> briser—je résiste—

> briser le réseau de
> nos peurs entrecroisées, monter de notre rire, de notre
> mort—
>   jaillir de nos cadavres accouplés—
>   tel un
> funambule enfant au dessus d'un brasier froid,—qu'il
> rallume en se perdant . . . (pp. 105-106)

Long (far too long to be quoted in full or analyzed in detail
here), complex and extremely ambitious, "Un Récit" merges
theory of literature with imaginative literature in ways that
eclipse the poet's previous efforts in this mode, including
Moraines. In fact, "Un Récit" may be the most perfect blend of
method and adventure yet written by any of the poets treated
in this book. The title itself exemplifies this fusion and hence
merits special scrutiny. The term (and concept) "récit" has re-
ceived wide critical attention in recent years; Gérard Genette's
three-way breakdown of its main components seems especially
relevant here:

> . . . *récit* désigne l'énoncé narratif, le discours oral ou écrit
> qui assume la relation d'un événement ou d'une série
> d'événements. . . . *récit* désigne la succession d'événements,
> réels ou fictifs, qui font l'objet de ce discours, et leurs
> diverses relations d'enchaînement, d'opposition, de répéti-
> tion. . . . *récit* désigne encore un événement: non plus
> toutefois celui que l'on raconte, mais celui qui consiste en ce
> que quelqu'un raconte quelque chose: l'acte de narrer pris en
> lui-même.[14]

Genette goes on to propose that the word "récit" be reserved
for the first of the above applications, "histoire" for the second
and "narration" for the third. He uses "récit" in its restricted
sense to refer to "le signifiant, énoncé, discours ou texte nar-
ratif lui-même." With "histoire" he would designate "le
signifié ou contenu narratif," while "narration" in his scheme

applies to "l'énonciation" or "l'acte narratif producteur" (p. 72). To a large extent, Dupin's poem defines itself in terms of the interplay within it of the three distinct meanings or functions which, thanks to Genette (and others), the contemporary reader has come to associate with "récit," for "Un Récit" is at once a text, a story and an act of recounting.

But Dupin exploits still other notions that are triggered by his title. First of all, in choosing as his title a term that announces the narrative mode, the poet effectively shortcircuits his reader's expectations. The name "Jacques Dupin" appearing in the review *Argile* (where "Un Récit" was first published) prepares the reader to encounter not a narrative but a poem. This interference with the reader's usual expectations is then compounded by the contradictory fact that the text itself is obviously closer to "poetry" than to "prose." The incongruity that exists between, on the one hand, the author's name and the magazine and, on the other, the text's title, an incongruity that is then followed by the clash of title and text, sets the reader up for an experience that will be both plural (i.e., open-ended) and theoretical (i.e., form-oriented). Dupin's obvious avoidance of more deeply entrenched generic terms for the narrative ("conte," "nouvelle," "roman," "histoire") does the rest; only "récit" can suggest something unfinished, unclosed, or the idea of a fragment of some larger whole (e.g., the "récit de Théramène" in *Phèdre*, the "récitatif" passages in grand opera). The ending of "Un Récit" underscores this connotation of the title even as it discourages any foreclosed reading of the text:

Il n'y a pas de fin, tout peut reprendre, s'écrire, s'enchaîner: le cri, le calme, le dehors . . . (p. 112)

In terms of textual density (or overdetermination), inner coherence (implying modification of the whole by a change in any part) and powers of self-generation, "Un Récit" rivals Ponge's "Le Pré." But it is perhaps less as a text than as a story, a sequence of events, and as a narrative act that "Un Ré-cit" recalls Ponge, and less the author of "Le Pré" than that of "Joca Seria" and "Réflexions sur les statuettes figures et pein-tures d'Alberto Giacometti." For one appropriate way to read "Un Récit" is as the transposition of Giacometti according to Ponge into Dupin according to Dupin. If Giacometti is the sculptor of the first person singular caught in the act of disin-tegrating, as Ponge would suggest, with "Un Récit" Dupin becomes the poet of that same crisis. Where Ponge's "Réflex-ions" on Giacometti culminate in a meditation upon the death agony of a capitalized *JE*, Dupin's text opens in that fashion:

> JE—dont la configuration se déplace et disparaît, au-dessus de nous,—ultime, ou fumée . . .
> je, trahi, chassé, reconduit à la frontière, absorbé par le récit, ou dissous dans son espace . . . (p. 97)

Among other things, "Un Récit" is the story of *je*'s traumatic realization that it exists only in discourse (as Benveniste, Jakobson and other linguists have maintained), that as a mere shifter or indicator (not unlike "maintenant," "tu," "ce") it has no fixed, external referent.[15] (Rimbaud's famous "je est un autre" may thus be considered the disguised verbal matrix of "Un Récit.")

In an important sense, "Un Récit" reads like a covert hom-age to Ponge. Though the older poet is never mentioned by name, his texts on Giacometti, as I have already suggested, function as virtual paragrams for "Un Récit." Also, indirect allusions to Ponge abound in Dupin's text. The many occur-rences of the word "soleil," together with the phrases "étoile en abîme" (p. 106) and "le sperme de l'écrit-soleil" (p. 111), echo Ponge's "Le Soleil placé en abîme." Dupin's thinly veiled incorporation of his own first initial (for "Jacques") into his text as the "défroque emblématique" of the "sujet oppressif" (p.104) reminds us of "Fenouil" and "Prêle," which play a similar role at the end of "Le Pré." His question "que faire de

sa langue . . . sinon la brancher sur d'anciennes histoires, l'en-
raciner à des mottes de terre calcinée et prête à reverdir" (p.
110) echoes sentiments Ponge has expressed in *Pour un
Malherbe* and elsewhere; the poet's tongue is plugged into the
single organism that all past writing forms. Like Ponge in "Le
Soleil . . . ,"[16] Dupin embraces the strictly physical origin and
end of writing. Working on the corpus of one's language
means working on and through one's body, perhaps destroy-
ing, at least contesting, both one's self and one's linguistic
patrimony:

> Car je travaille sur un corps—un corps, oubliez-le, dont
> je dois être à la fois le père, et le parricide
> un corps dans le mien que je sens tressaillir, se ramasser,
> s'apprêter à bondir—
>
> se jeter DEHORS (p. 108)

"Un Récit" is both the story and the acting out, the telling,
of the poet's self in the process of recognizing its alienation
from scriptural *je*, or rather of its finding itself invaded from
without by an alien sign: "tandis que le dehors dicte, que le
dedans crispé se dérobe, s'ouvre, fuse" (p. 101). As Jacques
Derrida has reminded us, writing has traditionally been con-
sidered an "irruption du *dehors* dans le *dedans*, entamant l'in-
tériorité de l'âme."[17] "Dehors" is the only word other than
"je" that is completely capitalized in "Un Récit"; it is the
word that concludes Dupin's text (in lower case) and it is the
title of the book in which "Un Récit" appears. I may think
that I invest every word I use with meaning, with my
thoughts, feelings and intentions, and the word "I" is espe-
cially precious to me as the vessel of my very self. In truth,
however, all words, including "I" or "je," pre-exist me and
surround me, *langue* comes before and presses in on *parole*. My
most intimate utterance is shaped from the outside (*dehors*). In
this perspective, Dupin seems ready to ally himself with
semantic materialists like Julia Kristeva, who hold that sig-

nification arises *outside* individual subjectivity, that it occurs in the practice, the production of the text.[18] Moreover, the specific meaning that "dehors" acquires in "Un Récit" suggests a convergence of preoccupations among Dupin, Kristeva and Derrida.

Such a convergence seems all the more plausible in the light of the demystified view of writing that Dupin expresses in "Un Récit." We like to think that a transcendent self or "I" controls the moving hand that writes, but the facts are otherwise, the writing writes itself, making do with that which is at hand, deploying its downstrokes ("jambages") according to what it encounters along the way:

> écriture balbutiante, éparpillée, interrompue, dont les jambages plient devant un accident minuscule, une pierre disjointe, un remous de l'eau du torrent . . . (p. 98)

The craft and not the craftsman performs:

> Un métier poursuit à l'écart son ouvrage inconsistant . . . (p. 99)

Poetry, as Jean Cohen points out, and as Dupin shows us in "Un Récit," "est faite tout entière d'écarts,"[19] it generates itself "par le scintillement de la surface, l'écart excédant l'écart" (p. 107). Writing is simply the reworking of clichés, such as that of the "belle inconnue" (pp. 100-101). The empirical "I" is absorbed, destroyed in the telling; to write is to rewrite and destroy. "Je" disappears into "récit" via "écrit" and "récrit":

> il écrit, au milieu du courant, le brouillon de ce qui aurait dû s'écrire innocemment, et qu'en le récrivant il détruit,—il détruit sans l'effacer . . . un récit? (p. 98)

The *je* of Dupin struggles against the *je* of the text, but Dupin's *je* loses and this is "le récit de sa perdition" (p. 107). "Un Récit," not unlike Ponge's "Le Pré," is thus a double story, one of death and one of birth; it recounts the death of the poet's historical self and the birth of this text, "pluriel splendide et affamé qui se dépouille de nos marques et de nos limites, comme un serpent de sa peau" (p. 111).

The most explicitly autobiographical section in "Un Récit" is reminiscent of *Moraines* and it occurs near the end of the text. In it, Dupin veers away from concerns that link him to semantic materialism and back toward his entropic origins in Reverdy, Giacometti and, especially, Char:

> J'attendais tout de la violence de l'oubli
>
> —l'articulation du récit, le pas suivant,—et de son jeu de trames et de chaînes, j'attendais, ici, par calcul, fourberie ou désir, que s'ouvre dans le réel un espace irréductible, une jouissance équilibrée, plus haute que la pleine mer, dont l'irruption, la fraîcheur . . .
>
> l'energie que je peux capter, produire, jaillir, au contraire, de la fragmentation, de la teneur de rapports fragmentaires,—d'un déplacement presque immobile d'éclats—
>
> implosion invisible de ce gisement vague et insensé, le ciel, inseminé par tous les pores de la surface, injecté jusqu'aux artères les plus arriérées du sous-sol (p. 110)

Expectation is countered and confounded by experience. Instead of the hoped-for opening in the real, the poet finds "fragmentation," "implosion." The general tone here, however, is affirmative: "l'énergie que je peux capter, produire, jaillir. . . ." Fragmentation is glossed, in Charian style, as "la teneur de rapports fragmentaires . . . un déplacement presque immobile d'éclats." Implosion itself has something heavenly about it ("implosion invisible de ce gisement vague et insensé, le ciel"). This positive note is entirely appropriate to Dupin's text as a whole and to its closing pages in particular, for in the final analysis "Un Récit," like all of Dupin's work since before *L'Ephémère*, celebrates man's fate as that of the eternal fabulator.

As celebrant of man's inexhaustible gift for fabulation, Dupin comes very close to, and possibly even succeeds in, reconciling the Orphic and the hermetic conceptions of poetry. For at bottom he "rewrites" not Reverdy or Char or Ponge, but all of these figures together. He thus serves as a kind of bridge between the means-oriented *L'Ephémère* (or *Argile*) poets and the end-oriented *telquelistes*. But with "Un Récit" in particular Dupin perhaps most of all rewrites Beckett, and less the entropic Beckett (of *Godot*, for example) than the Beckett whose "I" is forever fading into its "story," dies yet goes on and on in an endless rush of words, the Beckett of *L'Innommable*.

VI. Marcelin Pleynet

Marcelin Pleynet's poetry, collected to date in four volumes that appeared between 1962 and 1973,[1] exhibits over eleven short years such a rapid and specifically post-1960 evolution in mode and intent as to seem virtually a paradigm of the "future shock" that characterizes our time. In his ever accelerating disengagement from what he has come to perceive as a politically repressive and spiritually bankrupt culture, Pleynet embodies, to an exaggerated and hence clarifying degree, the rage, the brilliance and the singlemindedness of that generation of poets, critics and novelists who reached adulthood during the Algerian War (1954-1962), France's last gasp as a colonial power. For Pleynet and a number of his contemporaries, by the late 1960's it had become of paramount importance to act upon certain newly acquired but deeply felt convictions, among them that writing is neither an innocent nor a passive occupation, that language is neither a neutral nor a reliable reflector of some pre-existing reality, and that such traditional distinctions as those between meaning and expression, art and life, writer and revolutionary, are simply no longer permissible.

Because of his speeded-up, almost meteoric progression from gifted poet to revolutionary thinker, Pleynet recalls Rimbaud and Lautréamont, or, more precisely, popular conceptions of these figures. And certainly his 1967 book on Lautréamont encourages one to draw such parallels.[2] Yet with his first two and perhaps even three books, other, more predictable or at least more conventional filiations suggest themselves. At the same time it must be pointed out that the avowedly revolutionary and radically self-critical texts of *Stanze*, Pleynet's 1973 volume, in an important sense grow organi-

cally out of *Comme*, his metapoetic collection of 1965, and that
the texts of *Comme*, in turn, are rooted in a particular strain
that is discernible as early as 1962 in Pleynet's first book, *Pro-
visoires amants des nègres*. It is this phenomenon, the emergence
of what might be called Pleynet's style of total contestation,
including self-contestation, that I propose to examine in this
chapter. As we shall see, although he will eventually follow
the road to semantic materialism pioneered by Ponge and
taken recently, it would seem, by Dupin, Pleynet started out
not far from where Du Bouchet and Dupin began in the late
1940's.

Provisoires amants des nègres, published, as I have noted, in
1962, contains according to its title page texts that were writ-
ten during the years 1957-1959. Selected for the Prix Fénéon
in 1963, *Provisoires amants* in many respects typifies the poetry
collections of quality that have appeared in France since 1945.
The title, mildly shocking and playfully gratuitous, evokes the
latter-day Surrealism of recent decades. The poems themselves
confirm this initial impression through their deployment of
surprising, *non sequitur* images, accompanied by occasional hal-
lucinatory touches, and themes such as the intersubjective ex-
perience of love and the upstream quest for some pre-verbal
realm.

In other ways, too, *Provisoires amants* reveals a poet who be-
longs fully to a particular time, the post-World War II period.
Nietzsche and Heidegger furnish the book's epigraphs. Also,
certain models from earlier generations of twentieth-century
French poets make their presence felt. These include figures as
different from one another as St.-John Perse, Pierre Reverdy,
Paul Eluard, René Char and, to a lesser degree, André du
Bouchet. I refer to Pleynet's poetic ancestry and lines of filia-
tion not to dismiss him as merely derivative but in order to
show that at the outset of his career he is situated, on the de-
veloping arc of contemporary poetry, just about where one
would expect to find a talented poet who was born in 1933. In
time-honored fashion, Pleynet began writing, in his case dur-

ing the late 1950's, by ingesting the living tradition of French poetry so as to make it his own, transform it and, eventually, transcend it.

A poem like "Jabès" (p. 95), in its simplicity, its repetitions, its loving praise of the other, recalls many a poem by Eluard. "Quelle affamée" (p. 79) evokes the apostrophic celebrations and miniature seascapes of St.-John Perse's *Eloges*. The prose poem which begins "La jeune fille se retournait . . ." (p. 16) reminds us, if only fleetingly, of Char's "Congé au vent." Moreover, the imperious tone, intermittent though it is, of the twenty-six poem sequence entitled "La Cave natale" (pp. 31-59), suggests that Pleynet must at one time have been an avid reader of *Fureur et mystère*, an inevitability no doubt for a poet of his generation. But perhaps the most striking similarity between the author of *Provisoires amants* and another, older poet, involves Reverdy. The untitled verse poem that begins "à la nuit" could almost have come, at least in its first three stanzas, from *Les Ardoises du toit*:

à la nuit
l'ombre pâle pose la nuit
sur les choses mortes

tu ne sais plus tenir ton nom
et tu marches
tu marches sans souci des heures
vers la plus noire nuit

les herbes sont éteintes
en toi
la parole plus bas gagne la terre
et plus bas que la terre la mémoire

une racine te retient
pourtant plus jeune que l'arbre
un brouillard encore dans la nuit
parle d'un autre monde
     insignifié (p. 18)

The monochrome, stripped-down vocabulary, allusions to
death, night, impotence, extinction, phrases stressing the re-
centness of these states, the solitary walking figure, compara-
tives indicating diminution and movement downward—these
are some of the basic components of Reverdy's poetry. So basic
in fact as to make us suspect, if only for a moment, that "à la
nuit" may be a pastiche of Reverdy. On closer inspection,
however, it becomes clear that Pleynet actually moves away
from his elder in this poem, especially after the third stanza. A
fog-shrouded figure questing downward-backward in space-
time hears speech of another as yet unsignified world. The
vague terror that normally attends poetic closure in Reverdy is
not present here, and in its place we sense something hopeful
or at least positive, perhaps a hint of what Pleynet refers to
elsewhere in *Provisoires amants* as "ce point de lumière
ordonnée/que les grecs nommaient LOGOS" (p. 93).

Speech, or more often writing, though latent—even incom-
prehensible or indecipherable—substructures several texts in
Provisoires amants. In a remarkable renewal of the lost-love
motif, for example, Pleynet, in an untitled poem that begins
"Quelques ruines," transcends nostalgia by supplanting
Romantic elegy with an unselfpitying encoding-decoding of
love's former habitat:

Quelques ruines
la trace d'une rivière
nous retiennent ici

non pas un souvenir
mais une écriture

la phrase illisible que laisse dans la main
la lisière d'un corps aimé

la suie des mots qui brûlèrent ici
ruine de quel amour (p. 92)

The four-line poem entitled, significantly, "Ecriture" seems to equate writing with the flight of crows against the sun-filled sky or with the peasant tracing a furrow across a field:

> et dans le soleil
> un vol de corbeaux
> sur les labours
> derrière la charrue (p. 86)

But how far are we here in fact from Heidegger's metaphor for the thinker as one who traces a furrow in human language the way a peasant traces a furrow across a field?[3] Or, more pertinently perhaps for our present purposes, how far are we from the dominant imagery of *Dans la chaleur vacante*, the 1961 collection of another admirer of Heidegger, André du Bouchet? My point here is not so much that, along with Perse, Eluard, Reverdy and Char, Heidegger and Du Bouchet as well may have influenced or inspired Pleynet. Rather, I am suggesting that for his first book of poems Pleynet was writing, largely, the kind of poetry that would have been quite at home a decade later in the pages of *L'Ephémère*, the review that Du Bouchet, Jacques Dupin, Yves Bonnefoy, Michel Leiris and one or two other modernist or latter-day Surrealist poets were to bring out in the years 1967-1972. It was only in subsequent collections, especially in *Comme*, that Pleynet would adopt a post-modernist or programmatically metapoetic mode. However, the occasional concern with *écriture* in *Provisoires amants* indicates that even before 1960, the dawn of the *Tel Quel* era, Pleynet was perhaps ripe for a shift into that mode.

Pleynet's second book, *Paysages en deux*, published in 1963, in retrospect strikes one as a transitional work between *Provisoires amants* and *Comme*. Its first eight to ten texts, fragmentary readings of experience, both inner and outer, rather than the simple transcriptions they first appear to be, in a general way recall Reverdy. The similarity is particularly noticeable in a poem entitled "Un Brusque commencement" (p. 19), as well as in two untitled short pieces that begin, respectively, "Il fait sombre" (p. 20) and "Un regard" (p. 21). Further on in the volume we come across this untitled one-line poem: "A une rose je me noie" (p. 50); and at the bottom of the page we find this notation: "présence de René Char." Together, the line and the notation lead one to suspect that with this text Pleynet is offering us a highly compressed variant of Char's magnificent prose poem "Front de la rose."

Elsewhere in *Paysages en deux*, however, other, fundamentally different, exemplars can be detected. Now it is Wittgenstein, instead of Nietzsche or Heidegger, who provides the epigraph. And the book's second part, entitled "Les Lignes de la prose," is dedicated to Philippe Sollers, the animating force behind *Tel Quel* since the review's birth in 1960. It should also be noted that *Paysages en deux* was Pleynet's first book to appear in the "Tel Quel" series of the Editions du Seuil and that Pleynet joined the editorial board of *Tel Quel* approximately one year before *Paysages en deux* was published.

What all of this points toward is confirmed in many of the texts that make up this 1963 collection, namely that since 1959 Pleynet has moved toward a *telqueliste* or metapoetic mode in his writings. Literalism is more and more the order of the day (note, for example, the very title "Les Lignes de la prose"), as is wit that relies heavily for its effect on puns and other forms of word play. Both the title and the texts of the nineteen-piece sequence called "Proses d'identité" (pp. 93-111) illustrate this tendency. There is the amusing and highly effective rejection of the mimetic function of literary language in the poem "On ne peut plus supporter le réalisme" (p. 64), as well as in a text called "Récit" (p. 52) whose last line, "On ne peut manquer d'être surpris par son obscurité," expresses at once the poet's expectation and the reader's reaction to the poem. Thus in contrast to *Provisoires amants des nègres* where, despite occasional references to "logos" and "écriture," poetry still seems to function primarily as a means to an end and not as an end in itself, as a means of acceding to some absolute truth, state or realm, *Paysages en deux* comprises a number of texts that are autotelic, completely or almost completely turned in on themselves. It is this aspect of the collection that anticipates the dominant mode of *Comme*.

Before looking at *Comme*, we would do well to consider the opening statement in Philippe Sollers's review of this collection: "Osons dire ceci: le 'poète' qui refuse aujourd'hui de se voir écrivant des 'poèmes' a toutes chances d'être, en le sachant ou en l'ignorant, un mystificateur."[4] Thus, for Sollers, sustained self-consciousness has become the *sine qua non* of poetic composition. And, as he makes clear in the rest of his review, he admires *Comme* precisely because of the systematic way in which it folds back upon itself and in the process scrutinizes the very nature of metaphor, whose sign, as Sollers points out, is the word "comme."

In *Comme*, metaphor is not just the stuff of poetry, it is its sole subject. Pleynet begins exploring his subject in the epigraph, which, significantly, is drawn from the book itself, not from some "outside" source:

Deux pourtant quand bien même le nombre n'importe plus qui renvoie à l'unité

By its choice of words, word order and periodic style, this statement acts out exactly what it says, its form mimes its meaning. How does this iconicity, this coincidence of sense and syntax occur? First of all, the two adversatives in succession, "pourtant quand bien même," tend to cancel each other out, for normally the adversative serves to introduce an alternative, a *second* choice, hence to undermine or even deny whatever precedes it, what is *first* enunciated. Also, together in the sentence as they are, and with the second inflated from "quand même" to "quand bien même," the two adversatives, the two abortive *second* choices, subtly prolong and emphasize the sense of the first word, "Deux." Given such prominence in the sentence, the idea of two, or twoness, is in effect isolated, and thereby disengaged from the notion of one, or oneness. This happens also to be what the sentence says.

The periodic style reinforces the disjunction between two and one. "L'unité," oneness, is located at the farthest possible remove from "Deux." Also, Pleynet's choice of "l'unité" over the more expected "l'un" brings up so as to dismiss it the leveling, reductive power of analogical thinking. More effectively than the word "one" ever could, "oneness" or "unity" suggests the common ground, the single principle to which analogy reduces the endless diversity of human experience. Analogy flattens out disturbing uniqueness, hence difference, for the sake of smooth, reassuring similarity. Metaphor, on the other hand, allows difference to be perceived as sameness while still being perceived as difference, two to become one without ceasing to be two.

By his rejection of unifying analogy in favor of pluralizing metaphor, by his implicit criticism of any idealist-tinged nostalgia for some underlying, justificatory principle, by his philosophical and semantic materialism—traits and tendencies that are already evident in the epigraph to *Comme*—Pleynet recalls Francis Ponge. It seems no accident that at precisely the moment when Pleynet was writing *Comme*, Ponge's star was very much on the rise in *Tel Quel* circles. As I have already noted, texts by and about him were appearing regularly in the review; Sollers and Jean Thibaudeau were publishing books on him;[5] and Ponge was increasingly being recognized, to quote one critic, as the "living elder statesman" of the *Tel Quel* group.[6] And, most important in the present circumstances, Pleynet himself would dedicate his 1967 monograph on Lautréamont to Ponge.

An examination of one relatively short text from *Comme* will, it is to be hoped, let us see Pleynet at his Pongian, metapoetic best:

C'est toujours le même mot
mais pas ce qu'ils disent
ce qui nous inquiète
ainsi c'est toujours le même mot
et de temps en temps se lève une distance égale
non pas ailleurs non plus dans le regard
pourtant et comme la pensée les nomme
avec ces jambages/déployés dans l'apparence
où fuit et commence la pensée (p. 46)

In rhetorical terms the poem is organized roughly along dialectical lines, for each utterance after the first seems to correct or otherwise comment upon the one immediately preceding it. The expressions "mais," "ainsi," "et," "non pas," "non plus" and "pourtant" function as the basic pivots for the dialectical structure. The style, on the other hand, is essentially paratactic, in that the lines seem merely to follow upon one another rather than to build via explicit linkage toward obvious coherence. The text itself appears to describe phenomenologically the actual experience of reading, of reading generally but also of reading this text in particular. Words are more alike than unlike in their visual-graphic form if not in what they say. Meaning thus rests upon but the slightest of shifts within the near-perfect uniformity of what Pleynet elsewhere in *Comme* calls "toutes ces choses noires et blanches qui passent/sur la page où vous n'êtes pas" (p. 44). What is disquieting is the fragile, purely conventional basis of meaning. The absolute uniformity of the space between printed words, especially in a page of verse such as this one, epitomizes the absolute sameness that ever threatens to destroy the very possibility of deviation, hence of contrast and thus meaning. Reading, moreover, neither transports us elsewhere nor does it reside in our glance. And yet . . . In any event, thoughts that one has and words that one reads belong to the same, self-contained system— both inhere in "ces jambages/déployés dans l'apparence/où fuit

et commence la pensée." Downstrokes deployed like the slash
in the middle of the poem's second-last line occasion both the
death and the birth of all word-thoughts that can be read, but
especially of these word-thoughts that I am reading and creat-
ing here right now.

Reading "C'est toujours le même mot" we begin to under-
stand how the very act of reading deploys the downstrokes,
controls the flow and thus forms the writing. We also begin to
appreciate why metaphor obsesses Pleynet. For metaphor,
"comme," we now realize, is perhaps itself a metaphor for the
mechanism that silhouettes difference on the horizon of same-
ness, that lets shape rise out of the void. Metaphor may express
the experience that we have and that we make when sense and
nonsense play endlessly back and forth in the long read-write
of living-knowing, when consciousness is arrayed against itself
but not alienated from itself. As two in one and one in two, it
may well be the dyad of consciousness and self-consciousness,
perception and reflection, that defines human existence.

If Pleynet published his first three books of poetry in rapid
succession between 1962 and 1965, he brought out his fourth,
Stanze, after a hiatus of eight years in 1973. This does not
mean that following a sustained burst of writing Pleynet fell
into an inactive or fallow period. On the contrary, throughout
these years he continued his very active collaboration on *Tel
Quel*, where he was, and still is, *secrétaire de rédaction* and *di-
recteur de la publication*. Also, as I have already noted, he wrote
his monograph on Lautréamont during this time, and in 1971
his collection of essays in art criticism appeared.[7]

In his *Lautréamont par lui-même* Pleynet portrays Ducasse as
constituting a definitive break with the past, an end to a par-
ticular way of reading and writing. After Lautréamont,
Pleynet strongly implies, external, empirical reference will be
forever banished from literary language (pp. 68-71). He also
speaks in this study of "l'identité du lecteur et du scripteur"
(p. 112). Still elsewhere he casually remarks that "nous nais-

sons dans une langue" (p. 115). Whether he is referring to
Lautréamont as "rupture et fin" (p. 29), or maintaining that
the reader becomes "ce qu'il lit et ce qui est écrit: écriture" (p.
112), or asserting that our mother tongue is our native
habitat, Pleynet is echoing Pongian sentiments.[8] But this is
not surprising given the book's dedication and Ponge's appar-
ent sway over Pleynet during the writing of *Comme* just two
years earlier. What is surprising is that Pleynet removed his
dedication to Ponge for the 1970 reprinting of his book on
Lautréamont.

What happened between 1967 and 1970 that could have led
Pleynet to take this action? Quite simply, the events of May
1968, which in the years since then have had a continuing and
deeply politicizing effect on Pleynet and the entire *Tel Quel*
group. As a result of this politicization, Francis Ponge, along
with others, has been repudiated by *Tel Quel* for holding revi-
sionist, even reactionary, views and for being part of the liter-
ary and cultural establishment.[9]

Pleynet's re-evaluation of hitherto unexamined loyalties and
assumptions is reflected in *L'Enseignement de la peinture*, whose
two longest essays are devoted, respectively, to Matisse and
Mondrian. One of the effects of these essays, if not their pur-
pose, is to displace standard overviews of post-Impressionist
painting. This is particularly true of the piece on Mondrian,
"Mondrian vingt-cinq ans après" (pp. 99-126), where Cubism
is deliberately downgraded, and along with it Braque and
Picasso. The essay on Matisse, "Le Système de Matisse" (pp.
25-98), challenges in a more generalized but perhaps ulti-
mately more devastating way today's stock notions about yes-
terday's avant-garde. Simply by choosing Matisse over
Cézanne, Cubism's "official" forerunner, and by closely exam-
ining crucial turning points in Matisse's development, Pleynet
deftly shifts our attention away from those dates, periods and
paintings in the lives and works of Braque and Picasso that
have become such ingrained habits of mind as to seem virtually

synonymous with the milestones of modern art. On a less sub-
tle level Pleynet lets drop here and there throughout his piece
such remarks as "La pseudo-rationalité cubiste est réductrice"
(p. 50).

But what especially attracts Pleynet to Matisse is the paint-
er's lucidity regarding his own needs as an artist. According to
Pleynet, Matisse recognized the necessity of working system-
atically in order to let his unconscious impulses surface on the
canvas. He also believed that the male's deepest, most
thwarted, most sublimated impulse is the desire to couple sex-
ually with his mother, an angle of vision on Matisse that
Pleynet derives explicitly from his study of Freud. The poet is
evidently now ready to throw out, along with Ponge and the
Cubists, the incest taboo. He now holds that art generally is a
sublimated transgression of this taboo, and that writing
specifically is playing with the body of one's mother tongue. It
is in the spirit of transgressing such taboos, of overthrowing all
oppressive constraints, thus in the spirit of total revolution,
that Pleynet wrote *Stanze*.

The revolutionary program, almost overwhelming in its
sheer scope, that Pleynet envisaged for his 1973 volume is out-
lined in twenty pages of explanatory notes appended to the
main part of the book. In this appendix Pleynet informs us
that *Stanze*, subtitled *Incantation dite au bandeau d'or I-IV*,
comprises the first four out of a projected nine cantos (or
chants). He is attempting, he claims, to reveal "systématique-
ment le rôle incantatoire de la langue à travers les diverses
formes de civilisation et d'économie qui constitue l'évolution
de notre culture" (p. 153). To that end he is proposing "à
traverse l'aventure d'un sujet (l'auteur), la critique et les chants
des archaïsmes que notre culture continue de véhiculer" (p.
155). Pleynet's point of view in the cantos will thus be
oriented to and by economic history, his song will be both
critical and incantatory, and his vision will be consciously re-
fracted by the prism of his own "aventure" (thus again there

will be a major role, as in *Comme*, for a methodical self-consciousness).

The thought that we shall encounter in the cantos, according to Pleynet, will be " 'syntaxiquent' dialectique," and he goes on to state: "C'est systématiquement que j'ai opposé au martèlement conscient et inconscient d'un certain type de ponctuation syntaxique, la pensée et l'organisation de tout ce qui, pour l'occidental, fonctionne comme anomalie (balbutiements, jeu de mots, lapsus, rêve, argot, vocabulaire sexuel, etc.) . . ." (p. 159). Two points raised here deserve special attention. First of all there is the "Orientalism" implicit in the phrase "pour l'occidental." Elsewhere in *Stanze*, Pleynet's Sinophilia is more directly apparent, from the long epigraph in Chinese, through the lengthy explanation of the book's subtitle involving a Chinese legend, to scattered remarks about present-day China, including admiring references to Mao.[10] There is also in the passage just quoted an allusion to the ruptured syntax that Pleynet employs in the cantos, along with the implication that syntax reflects both conscious and unconscious mind. For Pleynet, the creative disordering of words can reveal the deep structure of both language and mind, and this disclosure, while undermining traditional conceptions of each, will ultimately overturn traditional conceptions of man and society as well. This is how radical literary practice and sociopolitical revolution converge for Pleynet.

The same disruptive potential of syntax lies behind Pleynet's growing interest in Joyce's *Finnegans Wake*, also discussed in the appendix. Significantly, the one statement by Joyce that is cited here also serves as the epigraph to the special Joyce issue of *Tel Quel*[11] that appeared within weeks of the publication of *Stanze*. This issue also carries "Joyce in Progress" (quoted in the "Introduction"), in which we find this assertion: "Or Joyce déplace en acte, en histoire, ce qui s'effectue de l'inconscient dans la langue" (p. 3), a characterization of Joyce that conveys very succinctly one of Pleynet's own hopes in writing *Stanze*. For with this work he aspires to a kind of "littérature d'engagement" in which language is no longer merely the instrument used for advocating social change but is rather the initial locus and primary source of all upheaval.

After the grand design set forth in the appendix, the cantos themselves, perhaps inevitably, come as something of a letdown. They contain, as Pleynet warns us in the appendix, "balbutiements, jeu de mots, lapsus, rêve, argot, vocabulaire sexuel, etc." They also contain marginal notations, maps, newspaper articles interrupting the text or in oblong boxes (or cartouches) running alongside, untitled inserts in a variety of languages, and the not quite readable photocopy of a long handwritten letter to the author from Philippe Sollers. Pleynet refers to these extra-textual elements as "collages" (p. 165). With the systematic syntactical discontinuities of the text compounded by these "collages," the reader is forced to maintain an open, tentative, pluralistic attitude toward the cantos.

In their format the cantos recall Pound, while in their genre they hark back through Pound and Lautréamont to Dante. But in their texture of deformation the specter of Joyce above all is called up, the Joyce who unleashes the disturbing, unsettling energy of previously untried combinations of letters, words and languages. Pleynet's non-literary gods, Freud and Marx, in addition to Mao, do the rest. All taboos, sexual, political, syntactical, are simultaneously or by turns transgressed.

The fourth canto seems a more effective "transgressor" than any of the earlier ones. This is perhaps because it is written largely as a series of satirical dialogues with numerous characters speaking the lines. A variety of voices call out to and argue with one another. Canto four thus exploits the essential ingredient of the dramatic form, conflict, to body forth Pleynet's syntactically dialectical thought. The earlier cantos, despite their *collages* and their repeatedly broken syntax, are borne ultimately on a single, plangent, albeit quasi-limitless voice, hence are basically lyric in form. Consequently they must strain to express endless rupture and contradiction.

The characters who appear in canto four are a mélange of historical, partly historical, imaginary and allegorical figures. Pleynet himself—that is, his persona—appears under the name of "Le poète." The brief excerpt that follows, taken from the middle of the canto, illustrates, I think, how Pleynet can orchestrate, with wit and to telling effect, a succession of dissonant voices:

Celeritas: Nouvelle langue et nouvelle coutume.
L'artiste: Qui l'entend?
Celer.: Tu l'entends.
L'artiste: Non tout est divisé et je n'entends plus rien. Il faut
    réunifier ou je reflète et je n'entends plus rien
Un militant: Curé!
L'artiste: J'ai mes opinions politiques
        j'ai mes dirigeants mes slogans mon parti
        je me cogne les enveloppes
        je colle les affiches
        pour ma liberté créatrice
Un passant: Ce sont les nouveaux surveillants!
Aristote: Et alors? Le maître ne s'affirme pas tel dans la pro-
    priété du capital donnant le pouvoir d'acheter du travail
    mais dans l'utilisation des esclaves. Pourtant il n'y a rien
    de grand ni de sublime dans cette science, ce que l'ouvrier
    doit savoir faire, l'autre doit savoir le commander. Là où
    les maîtres n'ont pas besoin de s'en charger eux-mêmes,
    l'honneur revient au surveillant, les maîtres par contre
    font de la politique et de la philosophie.
Tous: Oui! Oui! Il a pénétré dans nos veines et dans nos
    sabliers
Le poète: Toute ma littérature est de la cochonnerie
    et moi opportuniste
                le cochon d'Epicure
    C'est fini y'a plus rien
    C'est bonne broche je m'endors sans sommeil
    A moi la mort de l'art et le mot de la fin!

La femme: Donne moi du lard je te dis donne moi du l'art
Le militant: Y'a rien à faire c'est trop pourri! (pp. 137-38)

In this dialogue, philosophic idealism is confronted by materialism; smugness, by self-criticism; language as transparency, by language as opacity. Also, the poet engages his own past, including his existing *oeuvre*, in the processes of history. Finally, and perhaps most important, he undercuts the very possibility of uttering "le mot de la fin." Every word is provisional. Those words that would correct or refute previous words will themselves be contested and annihilated by words still to come.[12]

For all the break with the past that *Stanze* is supposed to represent, one may wonder whether its programmatic self-contestation differs fundamentally from *Comme*'s insistently self-querying nature, how far Pleynet has actually moved from metapoetry and his erstwhile mentor in that mode, Francis Ponge. The in-progress quality of *Stanze*, its openendedness, its self-correcting, work-book form, in these and other important features it resembles the kind of writing that Ponge has increasingly been engaged in since the 1940's. Also, the sexual dimension of writing surfaces here and there throughout Ponge, but especially in his discussions of "l'objoie," the metaphoric base of which is usually orgasm.[13] Finally, the title of the work, *Stanze*, as Pleynet explains in the appendix, is the plural of the Italian "stanza," whose first meaning is "séjour," "demeure," "logis." Only later does the idea of strophe enter the picture. Pleynet wants both notions, dwelling place and unit of poetry, as well as the broader concepts of space and time, to be kept in mind by the reader of *Stanze* (pp. 166-67). This is precisely the way one must read Ponge's dazzling "Le Pré," where place (the meadow) and word-particle (the prefix), as well as space and time, dance gracefully back and forth, now together, now apart, in a delicate, infinitely pleasurable ballet of signs and referents, signifiers and signifieds.[14]

Pleynet's is very much an "oeuvre en cours," a work in prog-
ress. Perhaps when the remaining five cantos of *Stanze* appear
he will have broken with Ponge and his pre-1968 past in deed
as he has already in word.[15] And maybe then he will be closer
than he is today to producing a synthesis of Joyce, Mao and
Freud, the goal that evidently spurs him on at this time.
Given the immense talent and extraordinary capacity for
growth he obviously possesses, it is not inconceivable that he
will one day realize his dream and write such a synthesis.
What is beyond question is that Pleynet's already completed
production telescopes over a half-century of the most advanced
French poetry, including the metapoetic efforts of the last dec-
ade. As for *Stanze*, whatever its shortcomings, with its almost
unprecedented breadth in form and in range of textual refer-
ence and with its relentless X-ray vision brought to bear
equally, across cultures and centuries, on humanity and the
self, it perhaps points toward the new, lyrico-epic mode of
writing that Philippe Sollers sees as next in line on his own
agenda, and as indispensable generally at this point in his-
tory.[16]

Afterword

Marcelin Pleynet, the youngest of the six poets treated in this book, perhaps most fully reflects its major concerns. His writings also suggest that there is as much convergence as divergence among the six figures. Ironically, this convergence becomes most obvious when one juxtaposes Reverdy and Pleynet, the two polar figures of the group in terms of age and basic conception of poetry.

A blatantly methodical adventure, a scriptural anabasis that advertises its self-regarding, self-constituting nature, Pleynet's *oeuvre* continues and broadens the metapoetic current in contemporary French poetry. Like Ponge's *Proêmes* and "Le Pré" or Dupin's *Moraines* and "Un Récit," *Comme* and *Stanze*, as we have seen, fuse imaginative literature with theory of literature completely; a questing poetic consciousness, quite paradoxically, unceasingly attends to its own elaboration. Thus Ponge and Dupin would doubtless agree with this simple but telling declaration in *Comme*: "Un livre tient un livre" (p. 61).

Yet it is precisely through *Comme* that Pleynet also links up with Du Bouchet, Char and Reverdy and, beyond them, with a kernel or nuclear element in Surrealist doctrine. For *Comme*, again as we have seen, amounts to a fragmentary but insistent meditation on the nature of metaphor and, by extension, on poetic consciousness as a heightened form of "normal" consciousness. Du Bouchet's obsession with the dyadic structure of consciousness, Char's exploitation of contradiction at every level of his writing and Reverdy's central theory of the image all valorize the notion of "twoness" as thoroughly as does Pleynet's poetic dissection of metaphor. All four poets view the coupling of disparates as the basic ordering or creative act of mind. Each in his own way thus shares André Breton's profound belief in the powers of *comme*:

Seul le déclic analogique nous passionne: c'est seulement par
lui que nous pouvons agir sur le moteur du monde. Le mot
le plus exaltant dont nous disposions est le mot *COMME*,
que ce mot soit prononcé ou *tu*. C'est à travers lui que
l'imagination humaine donne sa mesure et que se joue le
plus haut destin de l'esprit.[1]

If *Comme* is inconceivable without Ponge's example, and
Stanze without May 1968 (and the enormous discontinuity in
French intellectual history that this date symbolizes), Pleynet's
interest in the processes whereby the text comes into being, in
metaphor especially, is unthinkable outside of developments
in poetic thought that Reverdy's *Nord-Sud* essays helped set in
motion in 1917-1918. So much, at least, may be inferred from
a 1970 study by Pierre Caminade,[2] which opens (pp. 10-25)
with a close study of Reverdy's theory of the image, first enun-
ciated in *Nord-Sud*, and goes on to show how poets since Re-
verdy, including Pleynet (p. 52), have contributed to the care-
ful re-examination in our time of poetic means generally and
of metaphor in particular. The impact of Reverdy's concept of
the image on Breton (treated in Caminade, pp. 26-33) is well
known to readers of the first *Manifeste du surréalisme*. Largely
through Breton's reaction to his definition of the image,[3] Re-
verdy came to influence subsequent inquiry into the entire
analogical process, inquiry that eventually led to *Comme*.

In addition, following Apollinaire's lead, Reverdy with his
writings on Cubism, also begun in *Nord-Sud*, blazed another
trail that would later be taken by poets like Ponge, Char, Du
Bouchet, Dupin and Pleynet, that of *poésie critique*. Thanks to
Apollinaire and Reverdy, art criticism became an appropriate
(and an appropriated) genre for these poets to practice as a way
to enlarge the sphere of their esthetic and scriptural explora-
tions. It is in this fundamental sense that Pleynet's "Le Sys-
tème de Matisse" could not have been written had Reverdy not
written "Sur le cubisme" some fifty-four years earlier. What
becomes increasingly apparent in the light of these considera-

tions is that Pleynet, though riding with the vanguard of revolutionary scriptural activity, has roots in both the Surrealist tradition, broadly conceived, and the metapoetic current that flows out of Valéry and Ponge.

All of this suggests that Reverdy and Pleynet, as well as the divergent conceptions of poetry that they represent (the Orphic and the hermetic), may in fact be closer to each other than one would at first suspect. Indeed, that Reverdy chose to consign his reflections on poetry to essays and to restrict his analytical gaze to work already done, while Pleynet refuses to compartmentalize theory and practice in any fashion at all, is counterbalanced by the fact that both men gravitate toward some of the same speculative concerns and that for both the constant scrutiny of their work is an essential part of the enterprise of writing. Although reluctant to flaunt the artifice of the verse, Reverdy is clearly as methodical a poetic adventurer as Pleynet: "Il est . . . nécessaire de dégager nos moyens des oeuvres qui, déjà créées, nous ont été de fructueuses expériences."[4] In this perspective, it seems more than possible that the traces of *Les Ardoises du toit* visible in *Provisoires amants des nègres*, and to a lesser extent in *Paysages en deux*, bespeak an early influence that was after a time submerged but never really outstripped. More concretely, Reverdy's compositional ideal, formulated in the epigraph to *Le Gant de crin* (1927), "Je ne pense pas, je note," anticipates the recent radical shift in the locus or source of writing from the head to the hand, from self-expression to the self-generating text, and this veritable mutation in attitudes toward writing ultimately paved the way for *Stanze*. Thus from the ashes of Reverdy's disintegrating self rises the phoenix of Pleynet's self-forming/self-annihilating/self-re-forming text. It is within this context, and in this sense, that entropy foreshadows genesis.

Notes

INTRODUCTION

1. For instances of Ponge's use of this term, see *Tome premier* (Paris: Gallimard, 1965), pp. 220, 222.

2. Jean Hytier, *La Poétique de Valéry* (Paris: Armand Colin, 1953), p. 6.

3. James R. Lawler, *The Poet as Analyst: Essays on Paul Valéry* (Berkeley and Los Angeles: University of California Press, 1974), p. xi.

4. Guillaume Apollinaire, *Oeuvres poétiques*, ed. Marcel Adéma and Michel Décaudin, Bibliothèque de la Pléiade (Paris: Gallimard, 1956), p. 313. Adéma and Décaudin characterize "La Jolie Rousse" as Apollinaire's "testament poétique," p. 1113.

5. Guillaume Apollinaire, *Méditations esthétiques: les peintres cubistes*, ed. L. C. Breunig and J.-Cl. Chevalier, "Miroirs de l'art" (Paris: Hermann, 1965), p. 35.

6. "Une Aventure méthodique" was first published as the preface to *Braque* (Paris: Fernand Mourlot, 1949), pp. 9-61. It has been reprinted twice since then: in *Mercure de France*, 348 (juillet 1963), 363-92, and in Pierre Reverdy, *Note éternelle du présent*, ed. Etienne-Alain Hubert (Paris: Flammarion, 1973), pp. 41-104.

7. Marcel Raymond's *De Baudelaire au surréalisme* was first published by Librairie José Corti in 1933 and has been reprinted, often in revised form, at regular intervals since then.

8. Gerald L. Bruns, *Modern Poetry and the Idea of Language* (New Haven: Yale University Press, 1974).

9. This is one of the principal theses of Raymond's book. See especially the "Introduction" to *De Baudelaire au surréalisme*, pp. 11-46 (1952 edition).

10. Paul de Man, *Blindness and Insight* (New York: Oxford University Press, 1971), p. 172.

11. See Marcelin Pleynet, *Lautréamont par lui-même* (Paris: Editions du Seuil, 1967), and Francis Ponge, *Le Grand Recueil: Méthodes* (Paris: Gallimard, 1961), pp. 42, 203-5.

12. *Blindness and Insight*, pp. 174-82. Cf. Roger Shattuck's indi-

rectly supportive assertion that "Mallarmé, like Yeats, never lost touch with discursive thought, with the unity of a sentence," in *The Banquet Years* (Garden City, N.Y.: Doubleday Anchor, 1961), p. 336.

13. A. Kibédi-Varga, "Situation de la poésie française d'aujourd'hui (le poète et le réel)," *Neophilologus*, 49 (1965), 12.

14. Yves Bonnefoy, "La Poésie d'André du Bouchet," *Critique*, 179 (1962), 297. See also Du Bouchet's similar observations about language quoted in Serge Gavronsky, ed., *Poems and Texts* (New York: October House, 1969), p. 148.

15. The first issue of *L'Ephémère* contains essays on Giacometti by Bonnefoy, Du Bouchet, Gaëtan Picon and Michel Leiris, plus texts and designs by the artist. Nos. 8 and 18 contain additional designs by Giacometti, and No. 18 carries an interview with the artist conducted (some years before his death) by David Sylvester.

16. Three major works are Jacques Dupin, *Alberto Giacometti* (Paris: Galerie Maeght, 1964); André du Bouchet, *Alberto Giacometti, 1901-1966* (Paris: Galerie Claude Bernard, 1968); André du Bouchet, *Qui n'est pas tourné vers nous* (Paris: Mercure de France, 1972).

17. Gavronsky, *Poems and Texts*, p. 33.

18. *Tome premier*, p. 244.

19. Jean-Paul Sartre, *Situations*, III (Paris: Gallimard, 1949), 293.

20. Francis Ponge, *Le Grand Recueil: Lyres* (Paris: Gallimard, 1961), p. 73.

21. *Le Grand Recueil: Lyres*, p. 75.

22. Francis Ponge, *Nouveau recueil* (Paris: Gallimard, 1967), p. 94.

23. *Le Grand Recueil: Lyres*, pp. 75-76.

24. André du Bouchet, "Sur le foyer des dessins d'Alberto Giacometti," *Tel Quel*, No. 24 (1966), p. 16. It is perhaps appropriate to point out here that Du Bouchet has published in *Tel Quel* on one other occasion, "Poèmes," No. 8 (1962), pp. 45-46, the same issue in which Dupin's sole contribution to *Tel Quel* appeared ("Saccades," p. 47). Ponge twice published texts in *L'Ephémère*, "Nioque de l'avant-printemps," No. 2 (1967), pp. 49-59, and "L'Opinion changée quant aux fleurs," No. 5 (1968), pp. 3-29. While this

might suggest some commerce, albeit extremely limited, between the two reviews, it is no doubt more significant with regard to the actual relations between the two groups that the poets of *L'Ephémère* have published nothing in *Tel Quel* since 1966, and none of the younger figures presently or formerly associated with *Tel Quel* ever appeared in *L'Ephémère*.

25. Jacques Dupin, "Giacometti: sculpteur et peintre," *Cahiers d'Art*, No. 29 (1954), pp. 42-44.

26. The publicity brochure containing this statement may be consulted at the Bibliothèque Littéraire Jacques-Doucet, 10, place du Panthéon, Paris V.

27. Charles Davis, *The Temptations of Religion* (New York: Harper and Row, 1974), p. 22.

28. *Tel Quel*, No. 54 (1973), p. 3.

29. In *L'Enseignement de la peinture* (Paris: Editions du Seuil, 1971), pp. 24-126.

30. A quotation from Wittgenstein serves as the epigraph to Marcelin Pleynet, *Paysages en deux [suivi de] Les Lignes de la prose* (Paris: Editions du Seuil, 1963), while a line from Heidegger is the epigraph to the sequence entitled "La Cave natale" in *Provisoires amants des nègres* (Paris: Editions du Seuil, 1962), p. 31.

31. Wylie Sypher, *Loss of the Self in Modern Literature and Art* (New York: Random House, 1962), pp. 73-74. See also Robert Alter's illuminating remarks about the impact of the concept of entropy on modern literature in *Partial Magic: The Novel as a Self-Conscious Genre* (Berkeley and Los Angeles: University of California Press, 1975), pp. 142-43.

32. Samuel Beckett, *En attendant Godot* (Paris: Editions de Minuit, 1952), pp. 156-57.

33. See Pierre Reverdy, *Note éternelle du présent* (Paris: Flammarion, 1973), pp. 39-104, 155-88; Francis Ponge, *Nouveau recueil* (Paris: Gallimard, 1967), pp. 179-94; *Tome premier*, pp. 491-518; *Le Grand Recueil: Lyres*, pp. 80-87, 97-108; René Char, *Recherche de la base et du sommet* (Paris: Gallimard, 1965), pp. 49-60; Marcelin Pleynet, *L'Enseignement de la peinture*, pp. 25-98.

34. Gavronsky, *Poems and Texts*, pp. 145-46.

35. Jean-Paul Sartre, *Situations*, I (Paris: Gallimard, 1947), 248-49.

I. PIERRE REVERDY

1. Marie-Jeanne Durry, *Guillaume Apollinaire: Alcools*, II (Paris: SEDES, 1964), 172.

2. *Nord-Sud*, No. 1 (15 mars 1917), pp. 2-4.

3. Pierre Reverdy, *Le Gant de crin* (Paris: Plon, 1927), pp. 128-29. *Le Gant de crin* was reissued in 1968 by Flammarion, edited and containing an informative appendix by Stanislas Fumet.

4. See, for example, Reverdy's essay "Tradition," *Nord-Sud*, No. 13 (mars 1918), n.p. This article has been reprinted in Pierre Reverdy, *Nord-Sud, Self Defence et autres écrits sur l'art et la poésie (1917-1926)*, ed. Etienne-Alain Hubert (Paris: Flammarion, 1975), pp. 76-77.

5. See my monograph, *The Poetic Theory of Pierre Reverdy* (Berkeley and Los Angeles: University of California Press, 1967), esp. pp. 59-74.

6. Pierre Reverdy, "Le Rêveur parmi les murailles," *La Révolution surréaliste*, No. 1 (1er décembre 1924), pp. 19-20. This article was reprinted, with minor changes, in *Le Gant de crin*, pp. 11-17. See also Gaston Bachelard, *La Poétique de la rêverie* (Paris: Presses Universitaires de France, 1960), pp. 5, 9-14.

7. An essay by Reverdy entitled "Pablo Picasso et son oeuvre" appeared in the 14 December 1923 issue of *Paris-Journal*. It was reprinted shortly thereafter as the preface to *Pablo Picasso*, Les Peintres français nouveaux, No. 16 (Paris: Gallimard, 1924), pp. 3-14. The phrase in question, "il *imagine d'après nature*," appears on p. 8 of *Pablo Picasso*. This important essay has been reprinted again in *Nord-Sud, Self Defence et autres écrits*, pp. 185-207.

8. See, for example, A. G. Lehmann, *The Symbolist Aesthetic in France* (Oxford: Blackwell, 1950), pp. 85-104.

9. Stanislas Fumet, "Pierre Reverdy ou le lyrisme de la réalité," *Mercure de France*, 304 (1er novembre 1948), 439-52.

10. *Plupart du temps* (Paris: Flammarion, 1967), p. 175. *Plupart du temps* was originally published by Gallimard in 1945. The edition cited here, the first volume in Reverdy's *Oeuvres complètes* currently being issued by Flammarion, was edited and contains a useful appendix by Maurice Saillet.

11. Michel Décaudin, *La Crise des valeurs symbolistes* (Toulouse: Privat, 1960), pp. 19-21.

12. Olivier Hourcade, "La Tendance de la peinture contemporaine," *La Revue de France et des pays français*, No. 1 (février 1912), p. 40.

13. Guillaume Apollinaire, "Art et curiosité: les commencements du cubisme," *Le Temps* (14 octobre 1912). This article has been reprinted in Guillaume Apollinaire, *Chroniques d'art (1902-1918)*, ed. L. C. Breunig (Paris: Gallimard, 1960), pp. 263-66. The phrase in question appears in *Chroniques d'art*, p. 265.

14. Gérard Bertrand, *L'Illustration de la poésie à l'époque du cubisme 1909-1914* (Paris: Klincksieck, 1971), pp. 79-80.

15. The homage to Apollinaire and Reverdy's essay "Sur le cubisme" have been reprinted in *Nord-Sud, Self Defence et autres écrits*, pp. 13-21.

16. *L'Illustration de la poésie à l'époque du cubisme*, p. 79.

17. "Essai d'esthétique littéraire," *Nord-Sud*, No. 4-5 (juin-juillet 1917), p. 5. This important essay has been reprinted in *Nord-Sud, Self Defence et autres écrits*, pp. 39-47.

18. William Barrett, *Irrational Man: A Study in Existential Philosophy* (Garden City, N.Y.: Doubleday Anchor, 1962), pp. 216-17.

19. J. Hillis Miller, *Poets of Reality: Six Twentieth-Century Writers* (Cambridge, Mass.: Harvard University Press, 1965), pp. 7-8.

20. "Drame" was first published in *Nord-Sud*, No. 9 (novembre 1917), p. 10, and was reprinted in *Sources du vent* (Paris: Maurice Sachs, 1929) and later in *Main d'oeuvre* (Paris: Mercure de France, 1949). It is quoted here as it appears in *Main d'oeuvre*, p. 248. The definitive study to date of Reverdy as a Cubist poet remains Everett Franklin Jacobus, Jr., "Pierre Reverdy and the Poetry of Cubism: Literary Responses to a Revolution in Art," Ph.D. Diss., Cornell University, 1971.

21. *Nord-Sud, Self Defence et autres écrits*, p. 73. Etienne-Alain Hubert, editor of this volume, examines possible origins of "L'Image" (a discussion between Reverdy and Breton, two texts by Georges Duhamel) on pp. 280-83. Another line of thought that seems to parallel Reverdy's concept of the image can be found in Ezra Pound's definition of the one-image poem, first enunciated in 1914: "The 'one-image poem' is a form of super-position, that is to say, it is one idea set on top of another." See William Pratt, *The Imagist Poem* (New York: Dutton, 1963), p. 31. For a very suggestive (for Reverdy's theory and practice of the image) rapprochement between

Pound's theory of superposition and Sergei Eisenstein's notion of montage, all in the context of the Cubist perspective, see Wylie Sypher, *Rococo to Cubism in Art and Literature* (New York: Vintage Books, 1960), pp. 282-83. The Eisenstein "connection" is especially intriguing as regards both Reverdy's theory of the image and his poem "Drame" since the poet was enthusiastic about the great potential of movies. See his essays on the subject: "Cinématographe," *Nord-Sud*, No. 16 (octobre 1918), reprinted in *Nord-Sud, Self Defence et autres écrits*, pp. 91-94, and "L'Art du ruisseau," *Minotaure*, No. 1 (juin 1933), reprinted in Pierre Reverdy, *Note éternelle du présent*, ed. Etienne-Alain Hubert (Paris: Flammarion, 1973), pp. 223-27.

22. Pierre Reverdy, *Le Livre de mon bord* (Paris: Mercure de France, 1948), p. 73. Elsewhere in this volume other definitions of the poet also stress the idea of the poet as arranger, almost in a literal or even manual sense, of pre-existing verbal units: "Le poète est maçon, il ajuste des pierres, le prosateur cimentier, il coule du béton" (p. 91); "Le poète pense en pièces détachés, idées séparées, images formées par contiguité. . . . juxtapose et rive, dans les meilleurs cas, les différentes parties de l'oeuvre" (p. 132).

23. Pierre Reverdy, *En vrac* (Monaco: Editions du Rocher, 1956), p. 199.

24. *En vrac*, p. 139.

25. From a letter dated 16 May 1951 published in *Entretiens*, No. 20 (novembre 1961), p. 16.

26. *Plupart du temps*, p. 9. Subsequent page references to this volume are in the body of the text, preceded by *PT*.

27. See in *Plupart du temps* the following poems: "Envie," p. 11; "Les Cornes du vent," p. 16; "Carnaval," p. 18; "Le Patineur céleste," p. 26; "Après le bal," p. 42; and "Bataille," p. 47.

28. See in *Plupart du temps* the following poems: "Plus loin que là," p. 12; "Les Poètes," p. 19; "Salle d'attente," p. 22; "Incognito," p. 24; "Le Voyageur et son ombre," p. 27; "La Repasseuse," p. 28; and "Une Apparence médiocre," p. 30.

29. Albert Camus, *Le Mythe de Sisyphe* (Paris: Gallimard, 1942), pp. 28-29.

30. Jean-Paul Sartre, *La Nausée* (Paris: Gallimard, 1938), p. 166.

31. See Sartre's very pertinent remarks about the contemporary poet's necessary and highly original failure in "Qu'est-ce que la littérature?," *Situations*, II (Paris: Gallimard, 1948), 85-88.

32. See Anthony Rizzuto, "Metaphor in Pierre Reverdy's *Ferraille*," *Kentucky Romance Quarterly*, 22 (1975), 321-34.

33. "Sable mouvant" was first published in 1965 by Louis Broder in a deluxe edition illustrated by Picasso. It was reprinted in 1970 in the catalog for the exhibition "A la rencontre de Pierre Reverdy et ses amis" published by Maeght, pp. 15-22.

34. From a letter to Emma Stojkovic-Mazzariol dated 3 January 1948 published in *Mercure de France*, 344 (janvier 1962), 89.

35. *La Nausée*, pp. 217-21.

II. FRANCIS PONGE

1. Serge Gavronsky, ed., *Poems and Texts* (New York: October House, 1969), p. xi.

2. Francis Ponge, *Pour un Malherbe* (Paris: Gallimard, 1965), p. 203.

3. Pierre Reverdy, *En vrac* (Monaco: Editions du Rocher, 1956), pp. 181-82.

4. *Entretiens de Francis Ponge avec Philippe Sollers* (Paris: Gallimard/ Seuil, 1970), p. 14. Subsequent page references to this volume appear in the body of the chapter, preceded by *E*.

5. *Entretiens*, p. 48; Pierre Reverdy, *Nord-Sud, Self Defence et autres écrits sur l'art et la poésie (1917-1926)*, ed. Etienne-Alain Hubert (Paris: Flammarion, 1975), p. 133.

6. *Entretiens*, p. 169; *Le Livre de mon bord* (Paris: Mercure de France, 1948), p. 153.

7. Pierre Reverdy, *Cette émotion appelée poésie* (Paris: Flammarion, 1974), pp. 123-24.

8. Or as Michael Riffaterre has noted, Ponge's "descriptive poetry is not based upon direct mimesis, but upon an accumulation of verbal stereotypes." See "The Poetic Functions of Intertextual Humor," *The Romanic Review*, 65 (1974), 281, n.6.

9. Reprinted in Francis Ponge, *Tome premier* (Paris: Gallimard, 1965), pp. 383-415.

10. "Preliminary Notice," in D. H. Kahnweiler, *The Rise of Cubism* (New York: Wittenborn, Schultz, 1949), p. vii.

11. Two apiece have been reprinted in *Tome premier*, pp. 491-518; Francis Ponge, *Nouveau recueil* (Paris: Gallimard, 1967), pp. 179-94;

and Francis Ponge, *Le Grand Recueil: Lyres* (Paris: Gallimard, 1961), pp. 80-87, 97-108.

12. *Nord-Sud, Self Defence et autres écrits*, p. 199.

13. See Francis Ponge, *Le Grand Recueil: Méthodes* (Paris: Gallimard, 1961), p. 42; *Pour un Malherbe*, p. 140; and *Entretiens*, pp. 26-33, 94.

14. See Philippe Sollers, *Logiques* (Paris: Editions du Seuil, 1968), pp. 206, 217, 250-301.

15. *Le Grand Recueil*, 3 vols. (Paris: Gallimard, 1961); *Tome premier* (Paris: Gallimard, 1965); *Pour un Malherbe* (Paris: Gallimard, 1965); *Nouveau recueil* (Paris: Gallimard, 1967); and *Le Savon* (Paris: Gallimard, 1967).

16. *Francis Ponge*, Poètes d'aujourd'hui, No. 220 (Paris: Seghers, 1974).

17. (Paris: Gallimard, 1947), pp. 245-93.

18. See Jean Thibaudeau's brief but suggestive discussion of the basic difference between the texts of *Le Parti pris des choses* and Ponge's other (especially later) texts in *Ponge* (Paris: Gallimard, 1967), p. 112.

19. (Paris: Gallimard, 1943), pp. 597-99. See also Jean-Paul Sartre, *L'Idiot de la famille*, III (Paris: Gallimard, 1972), 47, for further revealing discussion of the status of language by Sartre, e.g., "Les mots écrits sont des pierres."

20. *Pour un Malherbe*, p. 306.

21. Gavronsky, *Poems and Texts*, p. 37.

22. Philippe Sollers, *Francis Ponge*, Poètes d'aujourd'hui, No. 95 (Paris: Seghers, 1963), and Jean Thibaudeau, *Ponge*, La Bibliothèque Idéale (Paris: Gallimard, 1967).

23. A comparable fascination with the "creative" potential of dictionaries is found in I. A. Richards' *Practical Criticism*: "No one who uses a dictionary—for other than orthographic purposes—can have escaped the shock of discovering how very far ahead of us our words often are. How subtly they already record distinctions towards which we are still groping. And many young philologists and grammarians must have indulged dreams of bringing some of this wisdom into the ordered system of science. If we could read this reflection of our minds aright, we might learn nearly as much about ourselves as we

shall ever wish to know; we should certainly increase enormously our power of handling our knowledge. Many of the distinctions words convey have been arrived at and recorded by methods no single mind could apply, complex methods that are, as yet, not well understood" (1929; reprint, New York: Harcourt Brace, Harvest Books, 1956), p. 208.

24. *The Voice of Things* (New York: McGraw-Hill, 1972), p. 19.

25. *Proêmes* has been reprinted in *Tome premier*, pp. 117-252. Subsequent page references to this volume are in the body of the chapter, preceded by *TP*.

26. Jean Thibaudeau, in *Ponge*, pp. 135-46, gives the dates of composition of all of Ponge's published pieces save "Fable" and a few others. However, like most of the other texts in the first part of *Proêmes*, "Fable" was presumably written sometime between 1924 and 1930.

27. The term "qualité différentielle" (as well as the idea that it expresses) appears in many of Ponge's texts but perhaps most tellingly in the essay entitled "My Creative Method"; see *Le Grand Recueil: Méthodes*, p. 42.

28. See "Francis Ponge's Untenable Goat," *Yale French Studies*, No. 21 (1958), pp. 172-81. "La Chèvre" has been reprinted in *Le Grand Recueil: Pièces*, pp. 208-13. Subsequent page references to this volume are in the body of the chapter, preceded by *GRP*.

29. See Thibaudeau, *Ponge*, p. 145.

30. *Le Grand Recueil: Méthodes*, p. 198.

31. *Le Grand Recueil: Lyres*, p. 81. The three-way breakdown of *Le Grand Recueil* (into "Lyres," "Méthodes" and "Pièces") indicates the three categories into which most of Ponge's writings fall. With the possible exception of *Proêmes*, his texts may generally be classified as occasional (e.g., essays on painters), methodological (i.e., essentially theoretical pieces) or imaginative ("créations métalogiques").

32. *Nouveau recueil*, pp. 203-9. The discussion that follows makes no pretense at being an exhaustive analysis of "Le Pré." Its primary focus, inevitably somewhat exclusive, bears on the text's principal metapoetic features.

33. *Le Savon*, pp. 127-28.

34. *Pour un Malherbe*, p. 60.

III. RENÉ CHAR

1. See Anna Balakian, *Surrealism: The Road to the Absolute* (New York: Dutton, 1970), p. 152, and Mary Ann Caws, *The Poetry of Dada and Surrealism* (Princeton: Princeton University Press, 1970), p. 17ff.

2. André Breton, *Manifestes du surréalisme* (Paris: Pauvert, 1962), p. 41.

3. Louis Aragon, "Une Vague de rêves," *Commerce*, No. 2 (automne 1924), pp. 89-122, esp. p. 122.

4. Pierre Reverdy, *Le Livre de mon bord* (Paris: Mercure de France, 1948), p. 12.

5. Breton, *Manifestes*, p. 27.

6. Reverdy, *Le Livre de mon bord*, p. 112. For a well-documented study of Reverdy's relations with the Dada-Surrealist group during the ten-year period following 1916, see Charles Bachat, "Reverdy et le surréalisme," *Europe*, No. 475-76 (1968), pp. 79-100.

7. *Entretiens de Francis Ponge avec Philippe Sollers* (Paris: Gallimard/Seuil, 1970), pp. 73-75.

8. *Entretiens*, p. 72.

9. Michel Beaujour, "Afterword: Text Without a Theory, Theory Without a Text," in Mary Ann Caws, ed., *About French Poetry from Dada to "Tel Quel"* (Detroit: Wayne State University Press, 1974), pp. 285-89.

10. *Entretiens*, p. 59.

11. Beaujour, "Afterword," p. 286.

12. From an interview conducted by Paul Guth entitled "Pour Pierre Reverdy, poète du présent, l'homme est imperfectible jusqu'à l'infini," *Le Figaro littéraire*, No. 524 (5 mai 1956), p. 4.

13. For a well-focused discussion of Char's Surrealist period, see Mechthild Cranston, "Violence and Magic: Aspects of René Char's Surrealist Apprenticeship," *Forum for Modern Language Studies*, 10 (1974), 1-18.

14. Virginia A. La Charité, *The Poetics and the Poetry of René Char* (Chapel Hill: University of North Carolina Press, 1968), p. 39.

15. Breton, *Manifestes*, p. 40.

16. Sarane Alexandrian, *Le Surréalisme et le rêve* (Paris: Gallimard, 1974), p. 9.

17. Georges Mounin, *La Communication poétique* (Paris: Gallimard, 1969), pp. 100-101. See also La Charité, pp. 48-57.

18. René Char, *Le Marteau sans maître* (Paris: José Corti, 1970), p. 41.

19. Mounin, p. 104.

20. *Le Surréalisme et le rêve*, p. 418.

21. René Char, *Fureur et mystère* (Paris: Gallimard, 1967), p. 67.

22. Char's obvious affection for and faith in words in their own right might remind one of Ponge. However, the younger poet's outlook is rooted in a fascination with an essentially synchronic phenomenon, semantic and phonic antitheses between and among words, while the older poet is drawn to words synchronically and diachronically, individually and in combination, and in their scriptural as well as semantic and phonic dimensions.

23. Martin Heidegger, *An Introduction to Metaphysics*, tr. Ralph Manheim (Garden City, N.Y.: Doubleday Anchor, 1961), pp. 106-13.

24. *Manifestes*, p. 342; *Entretiens (1913-1952) avec André Parinaud* (Paris: Gallimard, 1969), p. 99.

25. *Entretiens de Francis Ponge avec Philippe Sollers*, p. 105, and Albert Camus, *L'Homme révolté* (Paris: Gallimard, 1951), p. 97.

26. *Sept manifestes dada* (Paris: Pauvert, 1963), p. 35.

27. See *An Introduction to Metaphysics*, pp. 106-7.

28. See "Entretien avec Heidegger," *L'Express*, No. 954 (20-26 octobre 1969), p. 85.

29. See *L'Homme révolté*, p. 127; Albert Camus, "Carnets," *L'Herne*, No. 15 (1971), pp. 226-27; René Char, "L'Eternité à Lourmarin: Albert Camus," *Commune présence* (Paris: Gallimard, 1964), p. 163.

30. "A une sérénité crispée," *Recherche de la base et du sommet* (Paris: Gallimard, 1965), p. 132. Significantly, Yves Battistini's *Trois présocratiques: Héraclite, Parménide, Empédocle* (Paris: Gallimard, 1968), is dedicated to René Char.

31. See, in *Recherche de la base et du sommet*, "Héraclite d'Ephèse," pp. 90-92, and "Réponse," p. 113; see also Char's, "Partage formel," *Fureur et mystère*, pp. 67, 69.

32. In either one of two basic versions, "Commune présence" has been published a number of times since it first appeared in 1936 in

Moulin premier. Perhaps the clearest indication of its very special significance for Char is the fact that it is the title piece of his most ambitious anthology to date, *Commune présence* (Paris: Gallimard, 1964). I quote it as it has been most recently published in René Char, *Poèmes* (Paris: GLM, 1969), pp. 12-13.

33. "Partage formel," *Fureur et mystère*, p. 69.

34. "Les Premiers Instants," *Fureur et mystère*, p. 213.

35. "Partage formel," *Fureur et mystère*, p. 70.

36. René Char, "La Bibliothèque est en feu," *Les Matinaux* (Paris: Gallimard, 1969), p. 147.

37. "Le Rempart des brindilles," *Les Matinaux*, p. 116.

38. *Poèmes des deux années* is part of *Les Matinaux*; "Front de la rose" is on p. 123.

39. See, in *Fureur et mystère*, "Partage formel," p. 70, and "Feuillets d'Hypnos," p. 133; see also "La Bibliothèque est en feu," *Les Matinaux*, p. 146.

40. "Feuillets d'Hypnos," *Fureur et mystère*, p. 149.

41. See Edith Mora, "Le Théâtre solaire de René Char," *Liberté*, X, No. 4 (juillet-août 1968), 126.

42. See Georges Poulet's remarks on the importance of this image for Char in "René Char: de la constriction à la dissémination," *L'Arc*, No. 22 (été 1963), p. 43.

43. "A une sérénité crispée," *Recherche de la base et du sommet*, p. 126.

44. From Blin's untitled preface to Char's *Commune présence*, p. xvi.

45. *Aromates chasseurs*, p. 7. A number of texts from this collection, under the collective title "Aromates chasseurs," were first published in *Argile*, No. 1 (hiver 1973), pp. 6-24.

46. "Dans la marche," *Les Matinaux*, p. 196.

47. "Nous avons," *Les Matinaux*, p. 194.

IV. ANDRÉ DU BOUCHET

1. See "Introduction," n. 15.

2. Stephen Heath, "Trames de lecture," *Tel Quel*, No. 54 (été 1973), p. 5, n. 1.

3. Henri Meschonnic, *Pour la poétique*, II (Paris: Gallimard, 1973), 387-405. (The statement quoted appears on p. 388.)

4. Serge Gavronsky, ed., *Poems and Texts* (New York: October House, 1969), pp. 147-48.

5. Gavronsky, *Poems and Texts*, pp. 145-46.

6. Jean-Pierre Richard, *Onze études sur la poésie moderne* (Paris: Editions du Seuil, 1964), p. 237.

7. André du Bouchet, "Envergure de Reverdy," *Critique*, No. 47 (avril 1951), p. 308.

8. *Onze études*, p. 255.

9. Cf. Du Bouchet's use of the phrase "l'air bleu" in "Cession," *Dans la chaleur vacante*, p. 105.

10. Stéphane Mallarmé, *Oeuvres complètes* (Paris: Gallimard, 1945), pp. 369-70.

11. Yves Bonnefoy, "La Poésie d'André du Bouchet," *Critique*, No. 179 (1962), p. 295.

12. The second, third, fourth and fifth pieces, entitled, respectively, "Plus loin que le regard une figure," "Qui n'est pas tourné vers nous," "Figure" and "Tournant au plus vite le dos au fatras de l'art," were originally published in *L'Ephémère*, No. 1 (printemps 1967); No. 8 (hiver 1968); No. 11 (automne 1969); and No. 12 (hiver 1969).

13. *Poèmes de Hölderlin* (Paris: Mercure de France, 1963).

14. Quoted in Lawrence E. Harvey, *Samuel Beckett: Poet and Critic* (Princeton: Princeton University Press, 1970), p. 441. Cf. Giacometti's statement, "Art interests me very much, but truth interests me infinitely more," quoted (in English translation) by Hilton Kramer in "Alberto Giacometti's Moral Heroism," *The New York Times*, 18 January 1976, p. D 29.

V. JACQUES DUPIN

1. Jean Frémon, "La Nouvelle Poésie: Jacques Dupin," *Art et Création*, No. 1 (janvier-février 1968), pp. 16-20.

2. George Steiner, *Extraterritorial* (New York: Atheneum, 1971), p. 168, n. 9.

3. Quoted in Georges Raillard, *Jacques Dupin* (Paris: Seghers, 1974), p. 74.

4. *Times* [London] *Literary Supplement*, No. 3, 650 (11 February 1972), p. 146.

5. Under the title "Les Lignes de rupture," "La Ligne de rupture"

was first published in *L'Ephémère*, No. 15 (automne 1970), pp. 314-24. In slightly expanded form, it appears in Jacques Dupin, *Dehors* (Paris: Gallimard, 1975), pp. 9-21. The word "entropie" is found in *Dehors*, p. 17.

6. Jacques Dupin, "La Difficulté du soleil," *A la rencontre de Pierre Reverdy et ses amis* (Paris: Galerie Maeght, 1970), p. 13.

7. René Char, *Recherche de la base et du sommet* (Paris: Gallimard, 1965), p. 109.

8. Jacques Dupin, "René Char," *Exposition René Char* (Paris: Galerie Maeght, 1971), n.p.

9. Georges Mounin, *La Communication poétique* (Paris: Gallimard, 1969), p. 36.

10. Jacques Dupin, *Gravir* (Paris: Gallimard, 1963), pp. 87-88.

11. René Char, *Fureur et mystère* (Paris: Gallimard, 1967), p. 205.

12. Jacques Dupin, *L'Embrasure* (Paris: Gallimard, 1969), p. 46.

13. "Un Récit" was first published in *Argile*, No. 6 (printemps 1975), pp. 32-47. It has been reprinted in *Dehors*, pp. 95-112. All quotations are from *Dehors*.

14. Gérard Genette, *Figures III* (Paris: Editions du Seuil, 1972), p. 71.

15. See, for example, Emile Benveniste, *Problèmes de linguistique générale* (Paris: Gallimard, 1966), pp. 251-66.

16. Francis Ponge, *Le Grand Recueil: Pièces* (Paris: Gallimard, 1961), p. 187.

17. Jacques Derrida, *De la grammatologie* (Paris: Editions de Minuit, 1967), p. 52.

18. See the illuminating discussion of Kristeva's notion of semantic materialism in Oswald Ducrot and Tzvetan Todorov, *Dictionnaire encyclopédique des sciences du langage* (Paris: Editions du Seuil, 1972), pp. 449-53, esp. p. 451.

19. Jean Cohen, *Structure du langage poétique* (Paris: Flammarion, 1966), p. 152.

VI. MARCELIN PLEYNET

1. *Provisoires amants des nègres* (Paris: Editions du Seuil, 1962); *Paysages en deux [suivi de] Les Lignes de la prose* (Paris: Editions du Seuil, 1963); *Comme* (Paris: Editions du Seuil, 1965); *Stanze: Incantation dite au bandeau d'or I-IV* (Paris: Editions du Seuil, 1973).

2. *Lautréamont par lui-même* (Paris: Editions du Seuil, 1967).

3. See William Barrett's discussion of this metaphor in *Irrational Man: A Study in Existential Philosophy* (Garden City, N.Y.: Doubleday Anchor, 1962), p. 208.

4. *Logiques* (Paris: Editions du Seuil, 1968), p. 217.

5. Philippe Sollers, *Francis Ponge*, Poètes d'aujourd'hui, No. 95 (Paris: Seghers, 1963); Jean Thibaudeau, *Ponge*, La Bibliothèque idéale (Paris: Gallimard, 1967).

6. Serge Gavronsky, ed., *Poems and Texts* (New York: October House, 1969), p. 33.

7. *L'Enseignement de la peinture* (Paris: Editions du Seuil, 1971).

8. For Ponge's views on Lautréamont, see *Le Grand Recueil: Méthodes* (Paris: Gallimard, 1961), pp. 42, 203-5. For other aspects of Ponge's theory that anticipate Pleynet, see the rest of the volume just cited (*Méthodes*) and especially the excellent theoretical *mises au point* that Ponge has provided in *Entretiens de Francis Ponge avec Philippe Sollers* (Paris: Gallimard/Seuil, 1970).

9. Pleynet has set forth his reasons for repudiating Ponge in "Sur la morale politique," an editorial appearing in *Tel Quel*, No. 58 (été 1974), pp. 5-6.

10. For evidence of Pleynet's continuing and doubtless increasing interest in China, especially present-day China, see his "Du discours sur la Chine," *Tel Quel*, No. 60 (hiver 1974), pp. 12-20.

11. *Tel Quel*, No. 54 (été 1973).

12. Julia Kristeva—perhaps not surprisingly given her close association with Pleynet on the editorial board of *Tel Quel* and their common admiration for Lautréamont, who in their view embodies a revolution in poetic language—concludes her monumental thesis with a comparable deliberate assumption of the inherently provisional status of all utterance: "Une nouvelle taupe agit et ronge toute thèse." See *La Révolution du langage poétique* (Paris: Editions du Seuil, 1974), p. 620.

13. See in particular *Le Savon* (Paris: Gallimard, 1967), pp. 126-28.

14. See *Nouveau recueil* (Paris: Gallimard, 1967), pp. 201-9.

15. In *Tel Quel*, No. 58 (été 1974), as indicated in note 9, above. On the other hand, a more recent Pleynet text in *Tel Quel*, and one with a direct link to *Stanze*, suggests that the bond of common interests between Ponge and Pleynet is perhaps stronger than the latter

would care now to admit. See "Le Chant zéro" in No. 63 (automne 1975), pp. 86-104. In a brief preface to this text, Pleynet makes the following revealing statement: "Rédigé après une première lecture passionnée de Lucrèce, ce poème est selon moi une sorte de matrice de *Stanze*" (p. 86). As is well known among present-day French poets and critics, no writer, not even Malherbe, is as much admired by Ponge as Lucretius. See, for example, *Pour un Malherbe* (Paris: Gallimard, 1965), p. 322.

16. An interview with Sollers conducted by David Hayman, and translated into English with an introduction by Hayman, is particularly informative as regards this new form of writing. See "An Interview with Philippe Sollers," *The Iowa Review*, V, No. 4 (Fall 1974), 91-101. The following remarks by Sollers, for example, about (principally) his own recent evolution as a writer, are suggestive, it seems to me, of some of the changes that Pleynet has been attempting to effect in his writing since the late 1960's: ". . . while we must posit language as the locus of the literary act and even of thought, once this has been admitted, if we are inflexible on this point, everything will once more ossify, producing a pale monotony. Once again we will miss the most profound aspects of the literary experience. For example, what Joyce brought us in the way of a universal problematics, one which truly displays humanity while recounting the eternal return, one that in the process touches upon many, many events, becoming enormously inclusive. I think we are in a period when we must, and perhaps I am alone in doing this, we must insist on the need for a resurgence of these epic functions, and even of the lyric" (p. 100).

AFTERWORD

1. André Breton, "Signe ascendent" (30 décembre 1947), *La Clé des champs* (Paris: Pauvert, 1967), p. 135.

2. *Image et métaphore* (Paris: Bordas, 1970).

3. André Breton, *Manifestes du surréalisme* (Paris: Pauvert, 1962), pp. 34-35.

4. Pierre Reverdy, *Nord-Sud, Self Defence et autres écrits sur l'art et la poésie* (Paris: Flammarion, 1975), p. 40.

Index

PRINCETON ESSAYS IN LITERATURE

Adventures in the Deeps of the Mind: The Cuchulain Cycle of W. B. Yeats. By Barton R. Friedman

Shakespearean Representation: Mimesis and Modernity in Elizabethan Tragedy. By Howard Felperin

René Char: The Myth and the Poem. By James R. Lawler

Six French Poets of Our Time: A Critical and Historical Study. By Robert W. Greene

LIBRARY OF CONGRESS CATALOGING IN PUBLICATION DATA
Greene, Robert W.
  Six French poets of our time.

  (Princeton essays in literature)
  Includes bibliographical references and index.
    1. French poetry—20th century—History and
criticism.   I.   Title.
PQ441.G7   841'.9'1209   78-70297
ISBN 0-691-06390-7

During the last sixty to seventy years avant-garde poetry in France has evolved in two directions: one toward poetry conceived as a means to an end, the other toward poetry as an end in itself. Focusing on Pierre Reverdy, Francis Ponge, René Char, André du Bouchet, Jacques Dupin, and Marcelin Pleynet as the modern French poets who most faithfully reflect these directions, Robert Greene's chronological study allows us to follow the two-pronged evolution of French poetry since 1910.

Situating his argument in a detailed historical context and basing it on comparisons with artistic movements and the poets' own writings on art, and on extended analyses of selected representative poems, the author is able to establish a new intellectual-historical perspective on contemporary poetry.

Professor Greene finds that whereas Reverdy, Char, du Bouchet, and Dupin all embrace a conception of poetry as quest, as a search for the absolute, as the Way of beauty or truth, Ponge and Pleynet hold to a view of poetry as *fête*, as a celebration of the relative, as the play and display of language in action. What knits them together, he concludes, is the way in which each poet sums up his era as a stage in the development of twentieth-century French poetry.

Robert W. Greene is Professor of French at the State University of New York at Albany.